INTERMEDIATE COMMUNICATION GAMES

A collection of games and activities for low to mid-intermediate students of English

Jill Hadfield

Nelson

Thomas Nelson and Sons Ltd
Nelson House, Mayfield Road
Walton-on-Thames
Surrey
KT12 5PL   UK

51 York Place
Edinburgh
EH1 3JD   UK

Thomas Nelson (Hong Kong) Ltd
Toppan Building 10/F
22A Westlands Road
Quarry Bay
Hong Kong

© Jill Hadfield, 1990

First published by Thomas Nelson and Sons Ltd 1990

ISBN 0-17-555872-8

NPN 9 8 7 6 5 4 3

Permission to copy

The material in this book is copyright. However, the publisher grants permission for copies of the pages in the sections entitled "Games material" and "Rules sheets" to be made without fee as follows:

Private purchasers may make copies for use by their own students; school purchasers may make copies for use within and by the staff and students of the school only. This permission to copy does not extend to additional schools or branches of an institution, who should purchase a separate master copy of the book for their own use.

For copying in any other circumstances prior permission in writing must be obtained from Thomas Nelson and Sons Ltd.

Printed in Hong Kong

Contents

List of games	iii
Introduction	v
Teacher's notes	viii
Games material	26
Rules sheets	123
Structural index	128
Lexical index	128

Acknowledgements
I am very grateful to the staff and students of the Languages Section of South Devon College of Arts and Technology for providing a stimulating and creative work environment and a constant source of support, encouragement, inspiration and advice.

List of games	Function	Key structure
1 Tower block	1 describing habits	1 present simple
2 Whatsitsname?	2 describing objects	2 relative clauses
3 The three wishes game	3 expressing wishes	3 wish
4 Relatively speaking	4 defining	4 relative clauses
5 Lifeswap	5 describing lifestyle and habits	5 present simple
6 Matchmaking	6 describing character, tastes and habits	6 present simple
7 Whose?	7 describing people	7 whose
8 Alien	8 reporting past events	8 mixed past tenses
9 Sci-fi dominoes/Fairytale dominoes	9 narrating	9 mixed past tenses
10 Crossed lines	10 asking for information	10 question forms
11 Ideal homes	11 describing places	11 adjectives for place
12 Good news, bad news	12 reporting past events	12 past simple
13 Good intentions or The road to hell	13 stating intentions	13 going to
14 Future snap	14 future statements	14 future time clauses
15 Told you so!	15 giving advice and opinions	15 should, should have
16 Why not?	16 speculating	16 second conditional
17 Office politics	17 stating opinions	17 character adjectives
18 Yuck!	18 describing feelings	18 it makes me + adjectives
19 Sales reps	19 describing ability	19 will be able to, won't have to
20 Parent power	20 asking for and giving permission	20 past passives
21 Promises, promises	21 making promises	21 will
22 It wasn't me, Officer	22 describing experiences	22 present perfect
23 Guess what I've been doing!	23 describing recent activities	23 present perfect continuous
24 School reunion	24 describing past habits	24 used to
25 Lifemap	25 giving advice/talking about past possibilities	25 should, ought to, third conditional
26 Houseparties	26 making arrangements	26 will, going to, present continuous, would like
27 When did you last see your father?	27 talking about the past	27 past simple + ago
28 The queue	28 asking about the past	28 past simple, yes/no questions
29 Detective work	29 reporting past events	29 past perfect
30 Suggestive shapes	30 stating possibility	30 may, might, could
31 Tact	31 reporting what's said	31 reported speech
32 Yuppies	32 boasting	32 comparatives
33 Archaeologists	33 describing objects	33 it's + adjective
34 Crystal balls	34 making predictions	34 will have, will be
35 Christmas swapping	35 expressing likes and dislikes	35 like + -ing
36 Heads, bodies and legs	36 describing people	36 he's/she's + adjective
37 The adverb game	37 describing actions	37 adverbs
38 Boiled eggs	38 comparing and contrasting	38 comparatives, superlatives
39 Married life or Getting out of doing the washing-up	39 stating obligation	39 must, have to
40 The last game	40 thanking	40 thank you for -ing

For Sally
with love and thanks
in memory of Telexes to Lhasa,
and other editorial games

Introduction

1 About games

A game is an activity with rules, a goal and an element of fun.

There are two kinds of games: *competitive games*, in which players or teams race to be the first to reach the goal, and *co-operative games*, in which players or teams work together towards a common goal.

The activities in this book are *communicative games*, as distinct from *linguistic games*; that is, they are activities with a non-linguistic goal or aim. Successful completion of the game will involve the carrying out of a task such as drawing in a route on a map, filling in a chart, or finding two matching pictures, rather than the correct production of a structure. However, in order to carry out this task it will be necessary to use language, and by careful construction of the task it will be possible to specify in advance roughly what language will be required.

The emphasis in the game is on successful communication rather than on correctness of language. Games, therefore, are to be found at the fluency end of the fluency-accuracy spectrum. This raises the question of how and where they should be used in class. Games should be regarded as an integral part of the language syllabus, not as an amusing activity for Friday afternoon or for the end of term. They provide, in many cases, as much concentrated practice as a traditional drill and, more importantly, they provide an opportunity for real communication, albeit within artificially defined limits, and thus constitute a bridge between the classroom and the real world.

This suggests that the most useful place for these games is at the free stage of the traditional progression from presentation through practice to free communication; to be used as a culmination of the lesson, as a chance for students to use the language they have learnt freely and as a means to an end rather than an end in itself. They can also serve as a diagnostic tool for the teacher, who can note areas of difficulty and take appropriate remedial action.

2 About this book

The games in this book have been written for low to mid-intermediate learners of English. There is a range of difficulty, with some overlap between the more difficult games at the end of the *Elementary Communication Games* book, and the easier games in the *Advanced Communication Games*, though, as every teacher knows, games can be adapted up or down: a more difficult game may be a stimulating communication challenge for lower level students, requiring them to stretch the little language they have to the limit to complete the task successfully, while a relatively easy game that focuses on a particular structure may be useful even for advanced students as revision or error correction. In general, though, they have been written to fit in with the functions and structures that most students will encounter at intermediate level. Each game is written within a specific functional area and designed to practise a specific structure. They are not arranged in any particular order of difficulty: it is up to the teacher to select appropriate games to fit in with their own syllabus or textbook. However, the more difficult games (usually those where students are required to play a role, or to be more creative) are indicated by an asterisk in the teacher's notes.

The games are listed on the contents page under functional headings with an indication of key structures, but there is a comprehensive structural index for cross-reference at the back of the book. There is also an index to the main lexical areas covered in the games. Essential exponents and lexis for each game are listed in the teacher's notes, and the teacher should check that students are familiar with these before playing the game.

The games make use of a variety of techniques. Variety is important in language teaching, and a succession of games based on the same principles, though exciting and novel at first, would soon pall. Techniques used include information gap, guessing, search, matching, exchanging, collecting, combining, arranging, and card games, board games, problems and puzzles, role play and simulation techniques.

The simplest activities are based on the *information gap* principle. In these activities Student A has access to some information which is not held by Student B. Student B must acquire this information to complete a task successfully. This type of game may be *one-sided*, as in the above example, or *reciprocal*, where both players have information which they must pool to solve a common problem. The games may be played in pairs or in small groups, where all the members of the group have some information.

Guessing games are a familiar variant on this principle. The player with the information deliberately withholds it, while others guess what it might be.

Search games are another variant, involving the whole class. In these games everyone in the class has one piece of information. Players must obtain all or a large amount of the information available to fill in a questionnaire or to solve a problem. Each student is thus simultaneously a giver and a collector of information.

Matching games are based on a different principle, but also involve a transfer of information. These games involve matching corresponding pairs of cards or pictures, and may be played as a whole class activity, where everyone must circulate until they find a partner with a corresponding card or picture; or as a pair work or small group activity, where players must choose pictures or cards from a selection to match those chosen by their partner from the same selection; or as a card game on the 'snap' principle.

Matching-up games are based on a jigsaw or 'fitting together' principle. Each player in a group has a list of opinions, preferences, wants or possibilities. Through discussion and compromise the group must reach an agreement.

Exchanging games are based on the 'barter' principle. Players have certain articles, cards or ideas which they wish to exchange for others. The aim of the game is to make an exchange which is satisfactory to both sides.

Exchanging and collecting games are an extension of this. Players have certain articles or cards which they are willing to exchange for others in order to complete a set. This may be played as a whole class activity, where players circulate freely, exchanging cards or articles at random; or as an inter-group activity, where players agree to collect a certain set of articles as a group and then exchange articles between groups; or as a card game on the 'rummy' principle.

Combining activities are those in which the players must act on certain information in order to arrange themselves in groups such as families or people spending holidays together.

Arranging games are also sometimes called sequencing or ordering games. These are games where the players must acquire information and act on it in order to arrange items in a specific order. Items to be arranged can be picture cards, events in a narrative, or even the players themselves!

Board games and card games are familiar game types, where the aim is to be first round the board, or to collect most cards, or get rid of cards first. The cards and squares on the board are used as stimuli to provoke a communication exchange.

All the above activities may include elements of puzzle-solving, role play, or simulation.

Puzzle-solving activities occur when participants in the game share or pool information in order to solve a problem or a mystery — where did the aliens come from?, did Annie commit the murder?, etc.

Many games include an element of *role play*. Players are given the name and some characteristics of a fictive character. However, these are not role plays in the true sense, as the role play element is always subordinate to the game for the purposes of language use. The outcome of a game is 'closed'; once cards are distributed it develops in a certain predetermined way, while role play proper is open-ended and may develop in any number of ways.

Simulations — the imitation in the classroom of a total situation, where the classroom becomes a street, a hotel, or an office — are also used in the book, particularly in those games which practise interaction between the individual and services such as cinemas, theatres and estate agents. However, for reasons discussed above, these activities are simulation-games rather than true simulations since the outcome is again 'closed': students have a specific task or series of tasks to complete within the context of the simulation.

3 Some practical considerations

There are three main types of activity in this book: *pair work*, involving two partners, *small group work*, involving groups of three or four, and *whole class activities*, where everyone moves freely around the room. All these activities require some flexibility in the constitution of groups and organisation of the classroom. It is best to have the desks in a U-shape if possible. Students can then work with the person sitting next to them for pair work, and groups of threes and fours can easily be constituted by alternate pairs moving their chairs to the inner side of the U, opposite another pair. Whole class activities, which involve all the students circulating freely, can take place in the empty area in the centre of the U-shape. Simulation activities may involve special arrangements of furniture and suggestions are made in the teacher's notes for these activities. If it is not possible to arrange the desks in this way, this need not deter you! The traditional arrangement of front-facing desks can easily be adapted to pair work, with people at adjoining desks working together, while small groups can be formed by two people turning their chairs round to face the two people behind them. Whole class activities present a little more of a problem, but often there is a space big enough for the students to move around in at the front of the class, or desks can be pushed back to clear a space in the centre.

Games are best set up by demonstration rather than by lengthy explanation. The teacher should explain briefly what the game involves, hand out the photocopied cards, giving the students a little while to study them, and then demonstrate the game with one of the students in front of the class. It will be found that the idea of the game is probably easier for students to grasp from seeing the cards than from a verbal explanation, and that as they become more familiar with the idea of games and the techniques used, any initial problems caused by unfamiliarity will quickly disappear. Where more complicated card games are played in small groups, it is suggested that teachers hand out a photocopied rules sheet to each group of students together with the card(s). There is a reference in the teacher's notes for each game to indicate where rules sheets are provided. These are to be found at the back of the book, after the games material section.

Many of the games in this book involve role play. Role plays involve two distinct phases: preparation and production. In the preparation phase, students should be given sufficient time to digest the information on the role card and to ask the teacher for help with anything they do not understand. Some of the games have quite lengthy role cards that are almost mini-reading exercises in their own right, and students may find it helpful to make a few notes on the important points to help them focus on and remember the essential information. A list of 'essential vocabulary' — lexis that the students are likely to find difficult — is given in the teacher's notes for each game. In the role play games with long vocabulary lists however, students will not necessarily need to know *every* word on the list, just the ones on their particular role card. (They can then explain the meaning to other students during the course of the game.) If you have a large class, and the role play is to be done in two or more groups, it is helpful to put the students with the same role cards together in groups at the preparation stage to discuss the information on their cards and talk themselves into the role. When the students are sufficiently prepared, and all problems of comprehension ironed out, the role play can begin. Encourage the students not to rely too heavily on looking at their role cards, but to remember the information. With the shorter role cards, it is a good idea to collect these in before the role play begins; with the longer role cards, the students may feel they need to keep the notes they have made as a back-up, but they should be encouraged to internalise as much of the information as possible and to refer to the notes only if absolutely necessary.

The teacher's role in these activities is that of monitor and resource centre, moving from group to group, listening, supply any necessary language, noting errors, but not interrupting or correcting as this impedes fluency and spoils the atmosphere. It is a good idea to carry paper and pen and to note any persistent errors or areas of difficulty. These can then be dealt with in a feedback session after the game. In many cases, the game could then be played again with different partners or with different role cards. In other cases, mostly in those activities involving puzzle-solving, this will not be possible. However, a similar game with different information could easily be constructed to practise the same exponents, and suggestions have been made for this where appropriate.

The average time necessary for most of the games is 20-30 minutes, depending on the number of students playing. However, it is often possible to extend the game into a follow-up writing activity to consolidate the language practised in the game and suggestions have been made for this in the teacher's notes.

4 The role of games in the language programme

The inclusion of games as an integral part of any language syllabus provides an opportunity for intensive language practice, offers a context in which language is used meaningfully and as a means to an end, and acts as a diagnostic tool for the teacher, highlighting areas of difficulty. Last, but certainly not least, although the above discussion has tended to focus on methodological considerations, one of the most important reasons for using games is simply that they are immensely enjoyable for both teacher and student.

Teacher's notes

1 Tower block*

Type of activity
whole class
arranging

Function practised
describing habits

Exponent
present simple for describing habits

Lexical areas
academic subjects, hobbies, musical instruments, noises

Essential vocabulary
biochemistry, chemistry, biology, lit. (literature), geography, warden, philosophy, physics, PhD, architecture, anthropology, sociology, PE (physical education), engineering, politics, agriculture, oceanography, economics, geology, technology, saxophone, violin, guitar, double bass, cello, drums, droning, bleeping, yowling, thumping, vibration, grunt, yell, shouting, cheep, whistle, swearing, yapping, scream, barking, fitness freak/fanatic, opera buff, computer buff, folk dancing, unearthly hour, all hours of the day, a whole bunch, get worked up, just as well, keep the noise down, indescribable, get on with

How to use the game

The game can be played with between 7 and 46 students — the more the merrier! If you have a small class, it's a good idea to combine classes with another teacher for this game.

You will need a fairly large space for this game. If you don't have a large classroom or hall, it's best done outside.

Copy one role card for each student. The cards are printed in the order of the 'floors' in the tower block (page 1 = ground floor, page 2 = first floor, etc.) so if you have fewer than 46 students, make sure that you copy the cards in the order they are printed in the book (ie. if you have twenty-five students, use the first twenty-five cards).

You will also need to prepare up to seven large sheets of paper with the words, GROUND FLOOR, FIRST FLOOR, SECOND FLOOR, etc. written on them (depending how many students, and therefore floors, you have in the 'tower block'). These should be placed on the ground to indicate where the floors of the block are:

    etc.
   SECOND FLOOR

   FIRST FLOOR

   GROUND FLOOR
leaving enough space for students to assemble themselves in rows.

Give each student a role card.

Tell them they are all college students and live in a college hall of residence which is x floors high. They have information on the card about themselves and their neighbours above and on either side of them. Several of their neighbours have annoying habits.

Give them some time to read and absorb the information and ask you about problems.

The object of the game is for the students to use the information they have about their neighbours to arrange themselves in rows corresponding to the floors of the tower block. To do this, they will have to get up and move around the class, asking questions and describing themselves and their habits so that they find their neighbours, and then find the right place on the right 'floor'. (On every floor, there are about half the students who know the exact location of their rooms: the others should be able to locate themselves using them as reference points.)

When they are in the right places, ask them to complain to their neighbours about their annoying habits.

Note: You might like to check that they have all found the right place: a 'floor plan' of the building is at the end of the role cards section for quick reference. You can either use this to do a whole class check yourself, or cut it into 'floors' and give one strip to each 'floor' and ask them to check themselves.

2 Whatsitsname?

Type of activity
whole class or small group
collecting and exchanging

Function practised
describing objects

Exponent
*a thing which —s
a thing for —ing with*
relatives with end prepositions

Lexical areas
tools and utensils

Essential vocabulary
cut, open, join, screw, beat, hit, put, write, wash, make, turn, cook, dry, hold, paint, get out of, dig, contain, heat, water, grass, bottle, tin, cork, egg, wood, screw, nail, material, clothes, hole, food, flowers, hair, paint, fish, earth, tea, coffee, plants, letters, paper
Students do not have to know the names of the objects in the pictures before the game, but may like to learn them afterwards.

viii

How to use the game

This game may be played with from 6 to any number of players.

Version 1:
Copy one large picture for each student in the class. Then copy the smaller pictures, so that the objects in the smaller pictures correspond with the objects in the large pictures you have copied.
Give each student one large picture and four randomly selected smaller pictures.
The object of the game is for each student to collect four small pictures to correspond with the four objects on the large picture. To do this, they will have to move around the room asking other students for the things they require BUT *without mentioning the name of the object (even if they know it).* (Not 'Have you got a corkscrew?' but 'Have you got a thing for opening wine bottles with?'.)
If as student has a small picture corresponding to the object requested, it should be handed over. The game is finished when all students have the objects they require.

Note: To make it easier to see who has finished and who is left, ask students to sit down when they have collected their items and got rid of the cards they don't need (and give them a task to do to keep them busy and/or quiet, such as writing definitions of the objects they have collected).

Version 2:
Copy each large picture and each small picture once. Divide the students into six groups and assign each a different area of the classroom.
Give each group one large picture and four randomly selected smaller ones.
The object of the game is as above, but groups must negotiate with each other for the pictures they need. Each group is only allowed to send out and receive one 'ambassador' at a time.

Note: This version is easier to play with a large class, or where space is limited, but leads to less individual language practice.

3 The three wishes game

Type of activity
whole class
information search

Function practised
expressing wishes

Exponent
I wish I could…
I wish I had…
I wish I was…

Lexical areas
personal characteristics, talents and abilities, possessions

Essential vocabulary
as required by students: impossible to specify in advance

How to use the game

The game may be played with any number. Photocopy and cut up the 'granting cards' so that there is one for each student in the class. Put them in a hat or bag.
Give each student in the class a slip of paper and ask them to write three wishes on it, as follows:
I wish I could…
I wish I had…
I wish I was…
Ask them to fold it up and keep it in a pocket. Then pass round the hat or bag and ask each student to take one granting card.
Tell them that the card gives them magic powers to grant any wishes to do with that subject.
There is only one snag: they can't grant their *own* wishes!
The object of the game is to find people to grant their three wishes. To do this, students must move round the class, telling people their wishes until they find someone who can grant them. When they have had all their wishes granted, they can sit down.

4 Relatively speaking

Type of activity
small group
guessing card game

Function practised
defining

Exponent
…a person who…
…a machine which…
…a place where…

Lexical areas
occupations, places, machines and tools

Essential vocabulary
doctor, pilot, policeman, teacher, dentist, postman, fireman, astronaut, queen, church, hospital, library, school, post office, zoo, swimming pool, prison, vacuum cleaner, dishwasher, oven, washing machine, hairdryer, typewriter, calculator, lawnmower

These words should not be overtly pre-taught as that would 'give the game away'. It would be better if possible to introduce any unfamiliar words in a different context or lesson.

How to use the game

Students play this game in groups of three or four.
Copy one set of picture cards for each group, and cut them up.
Copy a rules sheet (at the back of the book) for each group.
Students should place the picture cards face down in a pile in the centre of the group.
The first player should take the top card from the pile and look at it without showing it to the others. He/she should give a definition of the person, object or place on the card, but without mentioning the name, for example, *This is a place where you go when you're sick.*
The first player who guesses 'hospital' correctly gets the card.
If no one can guess, the player holding the card may keep it.
The object of the game is to collect cards. The player with the most at the end is the winner.
The 'language mileage' in this game will vary according to the level of the students playing it. For instance, it will probably be enough for low-level students to produce the above definition, but more advanced students will get more fun out of the game if they realise that they can prevent their opponents getting cards by giving more subtle definitions, such as, for the above example, *This is a place where nice people give you tea in bed.*

5 Lifeswap*

Type of activity
whole class
exchanging

Function practised
describing lifestyle and habits

Exponent
present simple

Lexical areas
home, daily life, feelings

Essential vocabulary
cottage, detached, semi-detached, tent, caravan, mansion, flat, plane, film star, tramp, circus, businessman, monk, pop star
Other vocabulary impossible to specify, as it depends on students' imagination.

How to use the game

The game may be played with any number of students.
Copy enough picture cards for there to be one for each student.
Give these out to the students and ask them to imagine that they are the person pictured on the card. Give them a little while to imagine what it would be like to be that person: what do they do every day?, what does the house look like inside?, etc.
Then tell them that they are fed up with their lifestyle as pictured on the card, and would like to change if possible.
Give them a little longer to work out exactly what it is that they dislike so much about their present lifestyle, and what they are really looking for in life.
Then ask them to go round the class and explain their problems to other people until they find someone with whom they would like to swap lifestyles.
The object of the game is to find someone with whom they can swap lifestyles. Only exchange is possible: you cannot just give away lifestyles.
When they have found someone with whom they can exchange lifestyles, they should sit down.

Note 1: At first people may be looking for a lifestyle which doesn't exist. The initial phase of the game, where players sort out which lifestyles are actually available and which are impossible dreams, may take a while. Eventually they will probably find they have to compromise…

Note 2: To occupy those who have finished first and are sitting down, give a writing task, for example a letter describing what your previous lifestyle was like, why you have swapped and what your life is like now.

6 Matchmaking

Type of activity
whole class
matching

Function practised
describing character, tastes and habits

Exponent
present simple

Lexical areas
hobbies and interests

Essential vocabulary
as required by students: impossible to specify in advance

How to use the game

Play this game with any number of students.
Copy twice as many cards as there are students in the class.
Put students together in pairs and give each pair four cards. Ask them to discuss the pictures on the cards they have been given and to fill in the details on the card, according to their impressions of the character in the picture.
Collect in the cards.
Divide the class into approximately 1/3 and 2/3.

Divide 2/3 of the class into pairs, and ask them to sit together at strategically placed desks around the room. (For example, if you have a class of 24, ask 16 of them to sit in pairs at 8 desks in different parts of the room.)
These students are the 'marriage bureaux'.
The remaining 1/3 of the students are looking for a partner.
Give these 'hopefuls' one card each (appropriate sex). Tell them to imagine they are the person on the card. Divide the rest of the cards equally among the marriage bureaux.
These represent the partners that the bureaux have on their books.

The object of the game is to find a suitable partner.
To do this the 'hopefuls' must visit the marriage bureaux, describing themselves and what they are looking for, until they are offered someone suitable.

Note: Some students will finish before others. Ask them to sit down when they have found a partner and to write a letter to a friend describing the new man/woman in their life.

7 Whose?

Type of activity
whole class
search

Function practised
describing people

Exponent
whose
present simple
wh — questions
yes/no questions

Lexical areas
family, hobbies, pets, likes and dislikes

Essential vocabulary
as required by the students

How to use the game

Play this game with any number of students. Make one copy of the questionnaire for each student in the class.
You can choose to:
a) leave the questionnaire completely blank so that the students fill in both names and information (in which case students will be asking *wh—* questions)
b) fill in the names of the students in the class, so that students have to find something out about specific people in the class (but make sure the students you specify do have brothers, dogs, heroes, etc!). In this case, students will also be asking *wh—* questions.
c) fill in the information, but not the names (for example,…*is a student whose mother has brown eyes*) so that students have to find the people described. In this case students will be asking *yes/no* questions.
When you have prepared the questionnaires, give one to each student in the class.

The object of the game is to complete the questionnaire. To do this, students will have to move around the class, asking each other questions until they have enough information to complete the questionnaire.
As they finish, ask students to sit down in pairs and give each other a quiz on the information they have gathered (for example *Whose dog is called Bonzo?*, *Tell me the name of the student whose pet hate is spiders*, etc.).

8 Alien*

Type of activity
whole class
information search role play

Function practised
reporting past events
describing objects and people

Exponent
past tenses, especially past continuous/simple contrast

Lexical areas
everyday (and not so everyday) activities

Essential vocabulary
flashing, humming, saucer-shaped, spaceship, planet, computer, keyboard, destroy, rocket, attack, diverted, uniform, spit, UFO (Unidentified Flying Object), frightened, whimpering, madwoman, whizzing, fire, land, fire brigade, overhead, shake, teasing

How to use the game

The game may be played with groups of 8-16 students. If you have more than 16 students, play the game in two or more groups.
Copy one role card for each student in the class. The first eight role cards are essential, the others are 'floaters', so make sure you include the first eight cards for any group.
Tell the students that something very strange has just happened: a UFO landed in their neighbourhood, remained there for a few minutes, and then took off again. They are all neighbours, who witnessed the landing: their role card will tell them what they saw and heard.
Give them each a role card and allow a few minutes for them to read and absorb the information and ask

xi

you about any problems.
Then tell them that the UFO has just disappeared and they have all rushed out of their houses to tell each other what they saw. Ask them to tell as many people as possible what they witnessed.
When they have finished, regroup the students into small groups of three or four and give them a questionnaire to discuss and fill in.
The object of the game is to complete the questionnaire, and find out where the aliens came from (Saturn).

9 Sci-fi dominoes/Fairytale dominoes*

Type of activity
small group
arranging card game

Function practised
narrating

Exponent
past tenses

Lexical areas
science fiction, fairytales

Essential vocabulary
1: *spaceship, planet, space, alien, explode, monster, volcano, cactus, crab, fog*
2: *wolf, princess, prince, tower, frog, castle, lake, island, forest, thunderstorm, eagle, dragon, carpet, magic, needle, dragon, witch, ring, river*

How to use the game

This game is played in groups of three or four.
Copy one set of cards (sci-fi or fairytale) for each group.
The cards should be dealt out equally to all the members of the group.
The first player begins by choosing a card from his/her hand and laying it down on the table as the first event of the story, describing as he/she does so, what happened in the story.
The second player should then choose a suitable card to follow on as the next event in the story, and lay it down on the table next to the first, narrating the next stage in the story.
The object of the game is to build up a co-operative story.
When all groups have finished their stories, they can visit each others' tables and explain the stories to each other.
The activity also leads nicely into a follow-up writing activity.
There is a rules sheet for this game at the back of the book.

10 Crossed lines

Type of activity
whole class
information search

Function practised
asking for information

Exponent
question forms

Lexical areas
entertainment and services

Essential vocabulary
performance, book (tickets), appointment, matinee, weekday, what's on, bookable, advance, on the hour

How to use the game

This game may be played with any number of students.
Copy enough task sheets for half the class, and enough information sheets for half the class.
Place the chairs around the room in pairs back to back. Ask half the students to sit on the chairs (one student to each pair of chairs).
Give these students one information sheet each.
Give the other students a task sheet each.
The object of the game is for these students to complete their task sheets *in order*.
To do this, they will have to go and sit on one of the empty chairs, and 'telephone' the stationary student behind them, beginning the conversation with, for example, *Hello, is that the Gaumont Theatre?*
If they get the right number (*Yes, can I help you?*), they should ask for the information they need and write it down on the task sheet.
If they get a wrong number (*No, sorry. I'm afraid you've got the wrong number, this is the station.*) they should apologise, 'ring off' and move on to another pair of chairs.
They must complete the tasks in order, so they cannot make two consecutive phone calls from the same place. Thus the student in the above example must find the Gaumont Theatre first and obtain the necessary information, before returning to the 'station' to ask any questions.
The first student to finish is the winner.

11 Ideal homes*

Type of activity
whole class
matching/simulation

Function practised
describing places/houses
expressing wants and preferences

Exponent
I'd like...
I need...
I'd prefer...
...would be better, etc.

Lexical areas
houses

Essential vocabulary
names of rooms, *grounds, secret, trapdoor, greenhouse, gymnasium, trapeze, sauna, aviaries, distorting mirror, booby trap, safety net, sauna, cages, safari, regal, extensive, ideal, converted, access, feature, magician, clown, lion-tamer, deposed, ornithologist, critic*

How to use the game

The game may be played with any number of students.
Divide the students into two groups: approximately 2/3 should be house hunters, 1/3 should be estate agents.
Copy one job card for each of the house hunters.
Copy a corresponding house card for each of the job cards:

Magician   : House 1
Clown   : House 2
Lion-tamer   : House 3
Ex-king   : House 4
Olympic swimmer : House 5
Film critic   : House 6
Acrobat   : House 7
Ornithologist   : House 8
Gardener   : House 9
Large family   : House 10

Copy an equal number of ordinary houses.
Make a sign for each of the estate agents.
Divide the estate agents into three groups, and assign them 'offices' in different areas of the classroom.
Give each 'office' a sign and deal out an equal number of randomly selected house cards to each office. These are the houses they have on their books.
Give each of the house hunters a job card.
Tell them to imagine that they are that person and are looking for a suitable house.
Give the estate agents a few minutes to look through and familiarise themselves with their house cards and to put a price on each house, and let the house hunters have a few minutes to dream up their ideal homes.
When they are ready, the house hunters can begin to visit the estate agents' offices to look for houses.
House hunters and estate agents have different objectives:
The object of the game for the house hunters is to find a house that is ideal for them.
The object of the game for the estate agents is to sell as many houses as possible.

When the game is over, you might like to check whether the house hunters did in fact get the most suitable houses, or whether they got 'fobbed off' by convincing estate agents.

12 Good news, bad news

Type of activity
Small group
matching card game

Function practised
reporting past events/talking about the past

Exponent
past simple

Lexical areas
everyday activities

Essential vocabulary
a cold, bunch of flowers, parcel, skiing, concert, tickets, snow, cancelled, party, marry, stereo, prize, meal, burnt, rain

How to use the game

This game is played in groups of three or four.

Version 1: Snap
Copy one set of picture cards for each group and cut them up.
The cards should be dealt out equally to all the players in the group.
The first player should produce a 'good news' (GN) card and lay it on the table, describing what happened, beginning *The good news is...* (for example, *The good news is, I decided to ask her to marry me*).
The other players should try to find the corresponding 'bad news' (BN) picture. The player who has the picture should lay it on the table, describing the bad news for example, *The bad news is, she refused*.
The player who produces the matching bad news can collect the 'trick'.
The object of the game is to collect as many 'tricks' as possible. The player with the most at the end is the winner.
At the end, the combinations the players made can be compared with the order on the original sheet.
There is a rules sheet (A) for this game at the back of the book.

Version 2: Quiz
Copy one set of pictures for each group, but do not cut them up.
Instead the sheets should be handed intact to one person in each group: the quizmaster.
The quizmaster 'reads' out the good news for example, *The good news is, I asked her to marry me*.

The others try to guess what the bad news is, for example, *The bad news is she didn't hear me/The bad news is I asked the wrong person/The bad news is she said yes*, and so on.

The quizmaster awards a point to the player who guesses correctly.

The object of the game is to get the most points.

This version works well with more advanced, or more imaginative students: it actually produces more language.

There is a rules sheet (B) for this game at the back of the book.

13 Good intentions *or* The road to hell

Type of activity
whole class
matching

Function practised
stating intentions

Exponent
I'm going to...
(I was going to)

Lexical areas
everyday activities

Essential vocabulary
smoking, drinking, eating chocolate, shouting, harder, work, nice, person, lose weight, decorate, tidy, exercise, travel, punctual, decisive, relaxed

How to use the game

This game may be played with any number of students.

Copy the 'good intentions' form for every student in the class.

Give out the forms to the students. Ask them to imagine it's New Year's Eve and they are making their resolutions for the New Year.

Ask them to tick off on the form the resolutions they are making for themselves and to add one more personal resolution on the last line.

Then ask them to go around the class asking other people about their resolutions and telling them about their own.

The object of the game is to find someone with at least three resolutions that are the same as yours.

When the students have found their match, ask them to sit down together and imagine the time is one year later.

Ask them to tell each other what they succeeded in doing and what they were going to do, but didn't.

14 Future snap

Type of activity
small group
matching card game

Function practised
talking about the future

Exponent
future time clauses
going to
present continuous
will
will be —ing
will have —ed

Lexical areas
everyday activities

Essential vocabulary
go ahead with, be ready to, make money

How to use the game

This game is played in groups of three or four.

Copy and cut up one set of cards for each group. The cards should be shuffled and dealt out equally to all the players.

Player 1 should begin by taking any first half sentence, reading it out and laying it on the table. The other players should try to find a second half to complete the sentence.

The first player to find an appropriate second half may collect the two cards and keep them as a 'trick'.

The object of the game is to collect as many 'tricks' as possible. The player with the most at the end is the winner.

Several combinations of half sentences are possible, though some are more 'likely' than others. To score a 'trick', the combination must a) make sense (for example, *As soon as I arrive, I'll tell him what I think of him* is possible, but *As soon as I arrive, I'll have left the country* is not) and b) be grammatically correct. In cases of dispute, the teacher should arbitrate.

There is a rules sheet for this game at the back of the book.

15 Told you so!*

Type of activity
whole class
information search role play

Function practised
giving advice and opinions

Exponent
should
ought to

should have
ought to have
will

Lexical areas
bad habits, personal disasters

Essential vocabulary
nothing in common, truant, expelled, engaged, bankrupt, rowing, nagging, divorce, in trouble with, prison sentence, shoplifting, gang, rough, debt, fiancee, little devil, rude

How to use the game

The game can be played with any number of students, but is probably best played in groups of 8 to 16. If you have more than 16 students make two groups.
Copy one 'now' and one 'one year later' role card for each student.
Copy one questionnaire per pair of students.
This game has four phases.

Phase one: Give out the 'now' role cards. Ask the students to imagine that they all work in the same place. It's the coffee break, and they are all bringing each other up to date with various bits of juicy gossip. Ask them to offer opinions to each other on what people should or shouldn't do about their problems.

Phase two: When they have all gone round and advice has been offered, seat them in pairs and give them a questionnaire to fill in together. They should discuss what the problem is, what should be done about it, and make a prediction as to what will probably happen.

Phase three: When they have finished, give each student the appropriate 'one year later' card, and ask them to go round as before, but this time with a 'told you so' attitude, commenting on what people *should have done*.

Phase four: When they have finished, put them back in pairs.
The object of the game is to discover how many of their predictions were correct.
The highest score wins.

16 Why not?

Type of activity
small group
guessing

Function practised
speculating

Exponent
second conditional

Lexical areas
everyday activities

Essential vocabulary
colour blind, abolished, banned, daylight, broadcasting, printing

How to use the game

This game may be played in groups of three or four.
Copy one set of statements for each group and cut them up.
Give three or four slips to each member of the group and ask them to complete the statements without showing the others. When they have finished, ask them to read out the first part of each sentence to the rest of the group, who must try to guess how they completed it.
If a player guesses correctly, they should be 'awarded' the slip of paper.
The object of the game is to collect as many slips of paper as possible.
The player at the end with the most is the winner.

17 Office politics*

Type of activity
whole class
information search role play

Function practised
stating opinions
describing character

Exponent
I think that...
In my opinion, etc.
adjectives for describing character

Lexical areas
character, talents and abilities

Essential vocabulary
punctual, efficient, inefficient, cheerful, grumpy, bad-tempered, hopeless at, precise, rigid, inflexible, flexible, organised, disorganised, decisive, indecisive, friendly, pompous, good-natured, down-to-earth, narrow-minded, kind, natural, careless, weak, open-minded, unpretentious, competent, miserable, standoffish, moaning, complaining, nice, shy, kind-hearted, forgetful, gentle, moody, muddled, tolerant, broad-minded, absent-minded, vague, rude, eccentric

How to use the game

The game may be played with 8-16 players. If you have more than 16 students, play the game in two or more groups.
Copy one role card for each student in your group/class.
If you play with 9 people, you will have to add the information about Gerry (just joined, very nice but

xv

rather shy) to Chris's role card. If you play with more than 9 you will have to add the information about the *last* person in the series to Gerry's role card, for example, if you play with twelve students then the last card in the series will be the twelfth card, Dani, and you will have to add the information about Dani (joined at the same time, nice, but absent-minded)to Gerry's role card.

You will also need sticky labels or pins for badges. Give out the role cards to the students. Ask them to make a badge for themselves with their name on. Tell them that they all work in the same office and that since their boss is leaving, one of them is eligible for promotion. Naturally, everyone has very strong ideas about who it should/shouldn't be, which they want to communicate to as many people as possible.

However, the rule is: you can say as much as you like about the people behind their back, but *never* to their face.

The object of the game is to find out what other people think of you.

You can either set a time limit on the game and when it is up, see how many people discovered anything about themselves and whether they discovered one opinion or two conflicting ones, or make a rule that as soon as people discover an opinion about themselves, they should sit down, out of the game. It then gets progressively harder for those that are left to find anything out. The aim of the game then is not to be left in until last.

18 Yuck!

Type of activity
pairwork/small group
information gap

Function practised
describing feelings

Exponent
It makes me + adjective
It makes me + verb (+adjective)

Lexical areas
feelings

Essential vocabulary
as required by students, but the following may be useful: *happy, sad, miserable, cold, drunk, excited, uncomfortable, laugh, cry, warm, hot, calm, nervous, tired, fat, hungry, bored, lonely, frightened, shiver, depressed, worried, anxious, lonely*

How to use the game

Version 1:
Students play the game in pairs.
Make one copy of the sheet of pictures for each student in the class.
Leave half the number of sheets intact, but cut up the others.
Divide the student into pairs.
Give student A the intact sheet of pictures, and tell him/her to look at it, but not to show it to student B.
Give student B the cut up pictures. Student A should describe his/her reaction to each of the pictures in order, for example, *It makes me sad*, *It makes me feel warm and happy*, etc.
Student B should select the pictures described by student A and arrange them in order.
The object of the game is for student B to arrange the pictures in the right order.
There is a rules sheet (A) for this game at the back of the book.

Version 2:
This version can be played in small groups of three or four.
Copy and cut up one set of pictures for each group. The cards should be placed face down in the middle of the group.
Player 1 takes the first card and describes his/her reaction to it (*It makes me happy, sad, fat,* etc.).
The others try to guess what the object is.
The player who guesses correctly may keep the card.
The object of the game is to collect as many cards as possible.
There is a rules sheet (B) for this game at the back of the book.

19 Sales reps*

Type of activity
whole class
matching

Function practised
describing properties and abilities

Exponent
will be able to
won't be able to

Lexical areas
everyday tasks and obligations

Essential vocabulary
as required by the students: words to do with household chores, office jobs and gardening may be requested

How to use the game

The game may be played with any number of students.
Divide the class into two equal halves: sales reps and buyers.
Copy three machine cards for each of the sales reps.

Give out the cards to the sales reps.
Give the sales reps five minutes to: 1 write down what the user of each machine will be able to do/won't have to do (for example, *You won't have to spend hours learning irregular verbs. You'll be able to speak fluent idiomatic English instantly.*). 2 give each machine a price (up to £1,000).
Give the buyers five minutes to write down three everyday problems. What would they like to be able to do? What would they like not to have to do any more?
Tell the buyers they each have £2,000 to spend on machines to improve the quality of their lives. They should go round explaining to the sales reps what they would like to be able to do/not to have to do any more, and the sales reps can tell them what the machines can do for them.
The object of the game is for the buyers to obtain the machines they want and the sales reps to sell all their machines.
The sales rep with the biggest profit at the end of the game is the winner.

20 Parent power

Type of activity
whole class/large group
arranging

Function practised
asking for and giving permission and prohibiting

Exponent
past passives

Lexical areas
childhood activities

Essential vocabulary
sent to bed, have a day off, pocket money, smack

How to use the game

This game works best with groups of about 8-10 people, though if you have a small class (up to about 16) you can do it with the whole class.
Make one copy of the questionnaire for each person in the class.
Give out the questionnaires and ask the students to fill them in.
Then put them together in groups of about 8-10 people and ask them to line themselves up in order, according to who had the strictest parents.
The object of the game is to find out who had the strictest upbringing.

21 Promises, promises

Type of activity
small group
exchanging role play

Function practised
making promises

Exponent
will

Lexical areas
family life

Essential vocabulary
moaning, can't stand, pick up, give a lift, fence, chop, weed, attic

How to use the game

This game is played in groups of 6-8. For groups of 6 leave out Auntie Joan and Susie. For groups of 7 leave out Susie.
Copy one set of role cards for each group.
Give the role cards to the students and tell them that they are all members of a family. Every member of the family wants the other members to promise to do something.
The object of the game is to extract the four promises.
The rule is, you must promise to do something only if you are promised something in return.

22 It wasn't me, Officer*

Type of activity
whole class
information search role play

Function practised
describing past experiences

Exponent
past tenses
present perfect

Lexical areas
interests, hobbies, travel

Essential vocabulary
opera, jewellery, jazz, lion cub, koala, antiques, smuggler, bird-watching, skiing, ski pass, mountain walking, incriminating, burglar, suspect (v)

How to use the game

This game may be played with any number of people.
Copy one role card for every member of the class, ensuring that as far as possible, every 'thief' card has a corresponding 'police' card.
Give out the cards.
Don't mention the words thief or police to the students, but simply tell them that they are all at a party, where they know very few people and they have to introduce themselves and make polite conversation about their hobbies, interests and so on.

xvii

The object of the game is for the police to identify their suspects.
When they have all had a good chance to mingle, stop the game suddenly.
Ask the police to come forward and identify their suspects, giving reasons.
If a suspect is correctly identified, he/she must confess.

23 Guess what I've been doing!

Type of activity
small group
guessing card game

Function practised
describing recent activities

Exponent
present perfect continuous

Lexical areas
everyday activities

Essential vocabulary
muddy, peeling, sauna, black eye

How to use the game

This game may be played in groups of three or four.
Copy and cut up one set of cards for each group.
Place them face down in the middle of the group.
The first player takes one card, but must not show it to the rest of the group.
He/she should imagine they are the person depicted on the card and describe their appearance to the rest of the group, for example, *I'm crying*.
The rest of the group must guess what activity the first player has been engaged in, for example, *You've been quarrelling, You've been watching a sad film, You've been peeling onions*.
The player who guesses correctly is allowed to keep the card.
The object of the game is to collect the most cards.
There is a rules sheet for this game at the back of the book.

24 School reunion

Type of activity
Large group/whole class
information search role play

Function practised
describing past habits

Exponent
used to
present tenses

Lexical areas
habits, jobs, school life

Essential vocabulary
chewing gum, bike sheds, paper darts, share, fantastic, practical jokes, detention, chatting, tell tales, actor, businessman, dentist, model, politician, taxi driver, soldier, undertaker, vicar, dustman, TV interviewer, spy, pilot, accident prone

How to play the game

Play the game with 8-16 players. If you have more than 16 in the class, divide the class into two or more groups.
Copy one role card for everyone in the class/group.
It is important to copy the cards in order, so if you have 9 people in a group, use the first 9 cards, if you have 10, use the first 10 and so on. Also see note below.
Make one copy of the questionnaire for every three or four people. If your class/group is smaller than 16, cut off the questions which are about the role cards you are not using.
You will also need sticky labels or pins for badges.
Give out the role cards and ask each student to make themselves a badge with their 'name' on.
Give them a few minutes to read and absorb the information on the card, then tell them that they are going to a school reunion — twenty-five years on.
They are very curious about what happened to their old school mates, and should try and mingle and find out as much as possible about what people are doing now.
When they have finished gossiping, regroup them into threes or fours and give each group a questionnaire to fill in.
The object of the game is to complete as many statements as possible.
The group that can answer the most is the winner.

Note: Because of the way the game is constructed, if you play with more than 8 people, you will have to add a piece of information on one role card. For example, if you have a group of nine, no one will have any information about the ninth person, Chris, so you will have to add on one role card (any one except Chris's own) the information that Chris used to play practical jokes. If you have ten people, the information about the tenth person, Jan, will be missing and you will have to add that onto a role card. And so on up to the 16th person, Glen(da).(*Glen(da) used to be accident prone.*) It is always the information about the *last* person that is missing.

25 Lifemap*

Type of activity
1 small group:board game

2 whole class: information search

Function practised
1 asking for and giving advice
2 talking about past possibilities

Exponent
1 *What shall I do...?*
  You should/ought to...
2 *If I had..., what would have happened?*
  If I hadn't..., what would have happened?
  third conditional

Lexical areas
career choices, life decisions

Essential vocabulary
acrobat, policeman, bank clerk, office worker, filmstar, lawyer, politician, shelf stacker, artist, baggage handler, astronaut, tramp, millionaire, waiter, popstar, university, study, law, advert, spy, government, persuade, flying lessons, space, bored, business, nightclub, recognise, talent, art school, talent-spotter, extra, hand in notice, casino, licence, debt, sculptor, fiddling expenses, suspicious-looking, trapeze artist

How to use the game

The game is played in two phases, which practise different language. (It is possible to do only Phase one if all you want to practise is *should* and *ought to*.) Phase one is a board game played in small groups of three or four.
Phase two is a whole class information search activity.
Copy one board for each group and a couple of sets of career cards, which you retain. Note that the board in the games material section is printed on two pages. Either copy onto two A4 sheets and stick them together or copy the double spread onto an A3 sheet. You may also like to enlarge the board if your copier has this facility.
Copy another set of boards (normal size): one for each student and keep these for phase two.
You will also need dice and counters or coins for each group.

Phase one: Give out one board, dice and counters to each group.
The players should all place their counters on 'START'.
The first player should throw the dice and move the counter forward. When he/she comes to a decision square, he/she must stop, even if the turn isn't finished. He/she should ask the other players for advice on what to do. The direction he/she takes depends on the group consensus. (If there is a deadlock the teacher has the casting vote.) If the turn isn't yet finished he/she can move on the necessary number of squares in the direction chosen by the group. If the turn is finished, he/she will have to wait till the next turn, before moving on.
Then it is the next player's turn.

Players continue in this way, with discussion stops at each decision square, until they reach one of the circles at the end. They may then ask for the card with their number on and see what career they ended up with.
The aim of the game is to get to the end and discover what career you end up with.

Phase two: Now give the members of each group a blank board each, and ask them to write in the names of the careers of each group member in the appropriate circles. They will have between one and four circles filled in, depending on the group decisions in phase one.
The aim of the next part of the game is to fill in all the other circles.
To do this, students will have to move around the class asking other students what would have happened if they had made a different decision, for example, *If I had decided to open a casino with the chief cook, what would have happened?* or *If I hadn't married the one-eyed trapeze artist, what would have happened?* Students may not be able to get all the information, if there are roads that no one in the class took. In this case, they will have to ask you at the end of the activity, when you pull it together. This leads well into a follow-up writing activity ('Opportunities I missed').
There is a rules sheet for Phase one at the end of the book.

26 Houseparties*

Type of activity
whole class
combining role play

Function practised
making arrangements
inviting, accepting and refusing

Exponent
will
going to
present continuous for future arrangements
would like/would rather/would prefer

Lexical areas
holidays, leisure activities

Essential vocabulary
damp, offend, colleague, fed up, fancy, tactfully, fuss, a big do, the whole clan, folks, guy, in-laws, celebrate

How to use the game

This game can be played with a minimum of 12 students.
For 12 students copy the basic family role cards: Ethel, George, Jean, Pete, Rob, Sally, Paul, Sue, Edna, Jim, Nick and Avril.

For 13 add Mick.
For 14 add Mick and Sam.
For 15 add Mick, Tom and Maisie.
For 16 add Mick, Tom, Sam and Maisie.
For numbers over 16 add university students (up to four) and foreign students (any number).
You will also need sticky labels or pins to make name tags.
Give out the role cards to the students and give them time to read them and ask you about any problems.
Ask them to make a name tag each and to wear it.
When they are ready, ask them to get up and discuss their holiday arrangements with the other members of their family.
The object of the game is to find the people you want to spend Christmas with.
To do this, students will need to make (tactful) arrangements with a) the people they want to spend Christmas with, b) the people they don't want to spend Christmas with .
When they find people they would like to spend the holiday with, they should remain in a group. The groups should be as follows:
Ethel, George, Tom, Maisie (Tenerife)
Jean, Pete, Rob, Sally, Paul (Jean and Pete's house)
Sue, Mick, Sam plus up to five university students (skiing)
Edna, Jim (Wales)
Nick and Avril plus any number of foreign students (open house at Nick and Avril's)

27 When did you last see your father?

Type of activity
small group
card game

Function practised
talking about the past

Exponent
past simple + *ago*
When did you first/last...?

Lexical areas
everyday activities

Essential vocabulary
smoke, drink, phone, write, catch a train, go to a restaurant, eat spaghetti, have a cup of tea/coffee, shave, have your hair cut, swim, eat with chopsticks, go to the disco, watch TV, go to the cinema, go on a plane, get a bunch of flowers, get a letter, last month/week/year, two days/an hour ago, yesterday, etc.

How to use the game

This game may be played in groups of three or four.

Copy and cut up one set of time cards and one set of picture cards for each group.
Ask the students to deal out the time cards and put the picture cards face down in a pile in the middle.
Player 1 picks up a picture card and asks the player on his/her right a question beginning *When did you first/last...?* based on the picture (for example, *When did you last smoke a cigarette?*).
The player addressed must reply, using one of the time cards in his/her hand (for example, *Half an hour ago*).
The other players must decide if the answer is plausible or not according to their knowledge of the player.
If the answer is plausible — it doesn't have to be absolutely accurate, just plausible — (for example, *Ten minutes ago/This morning* for a smoker, or *Two years ago* for someone who has given up) then the player may discard the time card.
If the answer is obviously implausible they may challenge the player, who has to tell the truth, and retain the time card.
Then it is the next player's turn.
The object of the game is to get rid of the time cards.
The player who gets rid of his/her cards first is the winner. There is a rules sheet for this game at the end of the book.

28 The queue

Type of activity
whole class
arranging

Function practised
asking about the past

Exponent
past simple
yes/no questions

Lexical areas
everyday activities

Essential vocabulary
past and infinitive forms of following verbs: *talk, share, catch, eat, have, listen, save, ask, make, have to, smoke, buy, quarrel, drink, read, drop, break, sing, play, be, tell, write, discuss, offer, whistle*

How to use the game

This game may be played with 8-30 students. If you have more than 30 students, invent a few more cards, or play in two groups.
Copy one card for each student in the class. It is essential to use the cards in the order in which they are printed: ie. if you have 20 students, use the first 20 cards.
If you have fewer than 30 students, you will need

to amend the last card in your queue: delete or cut off the line beginning *The person behind you...* and write in instead *You were the last person in the queue. When you got to the ticket office, all the tickets were sold out.*
Shuffle the cards and deal them out at random to the students.
Tell the students that yesterday they were all queuing for tickets for a musical. They can remember who was in front of them and who was behind them in the queue, but not exactly where they were in the queue.
The object of the game is to reconstruct the queue as it was.
To do this, students will have to move around the class, asking each other questions about what they did in the queue yesterday, in order to find out who was in front and behind them, and eventually reconstruct the queue by lining up in order.
You will need enough space for your students to form a long line (though this can snake about a bit if desks and chairs are in the way) and you should designate a point (desk or table) to act as the box office, where the queue begins.
If you have more than 30 students and decide to do the activity in two groups, you can make it into a competition between queues (though you'd better have a large space — hall or playground — if you decide to do that!).

29 Detective work

Type of activity
small group
arranging card game

Function practised
reporting past events

Exponent
past tenses, especially past perfect

Lexical areas
everyday activities

Essential vocabulary
crime, committed, chatted, knock, neighbour

How to use the game

This game may be played in groups of three or four.
Copy and cut up one set of cards and one introduction sheet for each group in your class.
Put the students in groups of three or four, and give each group one set of cards.
Ask them to shuffle them and place them face down in the middle of the group.
Tell them that a murder was committed last night. An old lady was found dead in her living room. She had been hit on the head with a frying pan, and jewellery worth £10,000 had been taken from the house. The murder occurred between 7 and 10.30 p.m. One of the principal suspects is Annie Hudson, the district nurse, who has the key to the old lady's house, and who lives ten minutes' walk away. The cards contain details of Annie's movements that evening. The students should read them together, and try to work out if she could have committed the murder or not. Since the cards have been shuffled, the events will be in a muddled order. Students should turn up one card at a time from the pile, and discuss the probable sequence of events together.
The object of the game is to reconstruct Annie's evening and to work out if she could have committed the murder or not.
The group that finishes first is the winner.

30 Suggestive shapes

Type of activity
pairwork
information gap

Function practised
stating possibility

Exponent
It might be/It could be...
It looks like...

Lexical areas
everyday objects

Essential vocabulary
as required by students, but the following may be useful: *potato, stone, wool, string, cloud, hat, bone, eye, house, flower, sun, ball, banana, saucer, stick, snail, eggshell*

How to use the game

Students play this game in pairs.
Make one copy of the sheet of pictures for each student in the class.
Leave half the number of sheets intact, but cut up the others.
Divide the students into pairs.
Give student A the intact sheet of pictures, and tell him/her to look at it, but not to show it to student B. Give student B the cut up pictures.
Student A should describe each of the pictures in order by saying what it resembles, for example, *It could be a witch's hat, It might be a bone*, etc.
Student B should select the pictures described by student A and arrange them in order.
The object of the game is for student B to arrange the pictures in the right order.
There is a rules sheet for this game at the back of the book.

31 Tact*

Type of activity
small group
matching up role play

Function practised
reporting what's said

Exponent
reported speech

Lexical areas
neighbourly, marital and international disputes

Essential vocabulary
teenagers, chop down, complain, quarrel, occasionally, slump, telly, dispute, destruction, rainforest, damage, flooding, taxes, imports, economy, crippling, nuclear, border, ban, industry

How to use the game

This game may be played in small groups of three to five.
Three is the ideal number: one for each side of the dispute and one to carry messages, but groups of four or five can be managed by making one or both parties in the dispute consist of two students.
Divide the students into small groups and copy three sets of cards (neighbours, husband and wife and countries) for each group in the class.
Arrange the classroom if possible so that there are two rows of desks with a free space between them. Seat all the neighbours A in one row, and all the neighbours B in the opposite row, with the go-betweens standing in the middle.
Give out the cards: neighbour A, neighbour B and go-between.
The object of the game is for neighbours A and B to reach a satisfactory compromise.
The rule is that they cannot speak to each other directly, but must relay messages through the go-between.
When a group has reached a compromise, ask two of them to change roles, so that a different person has a chance to be the go-between, and give them the husband and wife cards.
When they have finished that, change the go-betweens again and give them the countries cards.

32 Yuppies

Type of activity
small group
arranging card game

Function practised
comparing (boasting)

Exponent
comparatives
—*er than*
more...than

Lexical areas
possessions

Essential vocabulary
fur coat, camera, swimming pool, yacht, jet, stereo, diamond ring, adjectives as required by students, for example, *expensive, big, intelligent, beautiful, nice*, etc.

How to use the game

This game may be played in groups of three or four. Copy and cut up one set of cards for each group. Ask the students to shuffle the cards and deal them out equally to each player.
The game is played like dominoes.
The first player simply lays a card (any card) on the table, saying something about the object, for example, *My car cost £50,000.*
The next player should select a card (any card) and lay it down next to the first card, making some point of comparison, for example, *My diamond ring was even more expensive than your car* or *My diamond ring is more beautiful than your car.*
The third player should then follow suit, (for example, *My daughter is prettier than your diamond ring*) and so on (*My dog has a nicer personality than your daughter*).
If the player cannot think of a comparison, the turn passes to the next player.
The object of the game is to get rid of the cards.
The player who finishes first is the winner.
The rules are : 1 you can't use the same adjective twice. 2 absolute nonsense, (for example, *My house is more intelligent than your car*) is disqualified, though zany comparisons (*My cat is a better companion than your wife*) are OK.
There is a rules sheet for this game at the end of the book.

33 Archaeologists

Type of activity
small group
guessing card game

Function practised
describing objects

Exponent
It's + adjective
It's made of...
It's used for...

Lexical areas
adjectives for size, shape, material

Essential vocabulary
long, short, round, thin, fat, square, cylindrical, spiral, —shaped, disc, rectangular, metal, plastic, paper, wool,

cotton, wood, glass, toy, ornament, brooch, religious, purse, decoration, implement, musical instrument, jewellery

How to use the game

This game can be played in groups of three or four. Copy and cut up one set of picture cards for each group.
Give out the cards and ask each group to lay them face down in a pile in the middle of the table.
Ask the students to imagine they are archaeologists in the year 5000 and the pile of pictures represent objects they have dug up. The objects are no longer used, so they may not know what they are.
The first archaeologist should turn up the first card and look at it, without showing it to the others. He/she should describe its appearance in detail to the others, without mentioning its name, and tell them what it was probably used for (according to the description on the card).
The other archaeologists should, if they recognise the object from the description, say what, in their learned opinions, it was used for.
The player who states the correct use may keep the card and take the next turn.
If no one guesses correctly, the first player may keep the card.
The object of the game is to collect the most cards.
If you have an imaginative/more advanced group you may like to cut off the data at the top of each card and get them to invent their own spoof uses for the objects.
This game leads well into a follow-up writing activity: describing the objects and their (spoof) uses, or making up descriptions of their own objects for other students to guess.
There is a rules sheet for this game at the back of the book.

34 Crystal balls*

Type of activity
whole class
matching

Function practised
making predictions

Exponent
will have
will be

Lexical areas
love, money, family life, travel, career, health

Essential vocabulary
as required by students

How to use the game

This game may be played with any number of students.
Divide the class into two: fortune tellers and fortune hunters.
Copy enough hunter cards for the fortune hunters and enough crystal balls for the fortune tellers, making sure that as far as possible, there is an appropriate crystal ball for every hunter.
Seat the fortune tellers behind desks in different parts of the room, and give them each a crystal ball.
Give the fortune hunters each a hunter card. Allow them some time to read the card and ask you about any problems.
Ask the fortune hunters to give back, or put away, their cards and the fortune tellers to turn theirs over so they can gaze into the crystal ball.
Then ask the fortune hunters to visit the fortune tellers and ask about their future, until they find a fortune teller who will give them the news they want to hear.
The object of the game is for the fortune hunters to find a fortune teller to tell them what they want to hear.

35 Christmas swapping*

Type of activity
whole class
matching

Function practised
talking about likes and dislikes

Exponent
like, love, interested in, hate, can't stand, etc.

Lexical areas
hobbies, sports, interests

Essential vocabulary
hiking, flower arranging, ballet, DIY, outdoor type, classical music, dreary, go down well, jazz, slim, tennis racquet, golf, opera, pop, saucepans, apron, frilly, glamorous, frivolous, tight (money), practical, gardening tools, houseplants, board games, underwear, knickers (to), computer bridge, chess, perfume, misunderstand, spices, watersports, snorkel, wetsuit, cookery, astronomy, astrology, abstract painting, handkerchiefs, videos, guitar, tone-deaf, genealogy/family history

How to use the game

This game may be played with any number of students.
Copy as many role cards as there are students in the class, ensuring that as far as possible, each card has its 'partner'.
Give out one role card to each person in the group and explain that in a few minutes they are due to meet people at a New Year party, where they will discuss Christmas and presents they received.

They should impart the information on their role card and their opinions about it to as many people as possible. Perhaps they will find someone who can help them.
When they have found the person who can help them, they can sit down together.
The object of the game (though don't tell the students that) is to find someone with whom they can swap presents.

36 Heads, bodies and legs

Type of activity
whole class
exchanging and collecting

Function practised
describing people's appearance

Exponent
He's/She's + adjective
He's got/She's got...

Lexical areas
clothes, parts of the body

Essential vocabulary
adjectives for size, shape, appearance, clothes vocabulary, parts of the body

How to use the game

This game may be played with any number of students.
Copy one whole person for each student in the class and cut into three parts along the dotted lines. Give each student a head and ask them to imagine what the rest of the person looks like.
Then give out bodies and legs at random.
Ask the students to get up and walk around the class describing the person they are looking for (or imagine they're looking for) until they find someone who can give them an appropriate body or pair of legs.
They should not show their cards to each other until they are almost sure that they have found the right card.
The object of the game is to assemble a whole person.

37 The adverb game

Type of activity
small group
guessing

Function practised
describing how things are done/actions

Exponent
adverbs

present simple

Lexical areas
everyday actions

Essential vocabulary
adverbs as on the cards, action verbs as required by students

How to use the game

This game may be played in groups of three or four. Copy and cut up one set of cards for each group. These should be placed face down in the middle of each group.
The first student takes the top card without showing it to the others.
He/she should give the others a clue to help them guess the adverb, for example, *You kiss someone like this*, *You speak like this to a deaf person*, *You stroke a cat like this*.
The others should try to guess the adverb.
They may ask questions: *Can you speak like this?*, *Can you walk like this?*, etc.
The player who guesses correctly can have the next turn.
The object of the game is to guess the adverb.
You might prefer to make your own adverb cards, if you have specific vocabulary you want your students to learn.
There is a rules sheet for this game at the back of the book.

38 Boiled eggs

Type of activity
small group
arranging and guessing

Function practised
comparing and contrasting
asking questions

Exponent
comparatives and superlatives
question forms

Lexical areas
habits, family, appearance, likes and dislikes

Essential vocabulary
runny, soft, hard, etc., adjectives of size, times of day

How to use the game

Divide your class into groups. If you have up to 16 students you can play the game in two groups; over 16 students, it's best to have 4 groups.
Give each group a 'criterion' and ask them to arrange themselves in a line according to the criterion you have given them. For example, if you have given them *How do you like your eggs boiled?*

they should arrange themselves in a line from runny at one end to hard at the other.
When they have sorted out the order, ask them to line up opposite the other group (or if you have four groups, have two sets of two lines) and try to guess why they are standing in that order.
The object of the game is to guess the criterion behind the order of the line.
You can repeat the game, with the students making up their own criteria for lining up.

39 Married life *or* Getting out of doing the washing-up

Type of activity
pairwork
board game role play

Function practised
stating obligation

Exponent
must, have to

Lexical areas
household tasks, appointments

Essential vocabulary
wash up, dry up, paint, mow the lawn, cook, shop, hang out the washing, lay the table, clear the table, vacuum, sweep, polish, clean the windows, water the plants, weed the garden, scrub the floor, dust, do the washing, peel the potatoes, make the beds

How to use the game

Students play this game in pairs.
Copy one set of cards, one set of diaries and one board for each pair.
Students will also need a dice and two counters or coins.
Give each pair of students a board, a set of cards and one diary each.
Tell them they are a married couple, who always fight about the housework. The object of the game is to try and get out of doing as many household tasks as possible.
Tell them to place their counters at 12 o'clock on the board, place the cards face down in the middle of the board, and to keep their diaries without showing them to their partner.
Student A throws the dice and moves the appropriate number of squares round the clock. He/She then picks up a card from the pile and requests student B to do that task, for example, *Darling, could you possibly do the washing-up?* or *Darling, I hate to remind you but it's your turn to do the washing-up* or *About time you did the washing-up for a change, isn't it?*
Student B consults his/her diary. If there is an appointment entered for that time, he/she can legitimately make an excuse. (*Sorry, I've got to go to the dentists.*) If not, he/she can agree to do the chore, in which case he/she collects the card and keeps it, or he/she can bluff and make up an excuse, for example, *Sorry, I've got to pick my mother up from the station in ten minutes.*
Student A must decide whether student B is bluffing or not. If he/she thinks B is telling the truth, he/she must keep the card. If, on the other hand, he/she judges that B is bluffing, he/she can challenge B.
If B is bluffing, B must keep the card *and* miss a go. If A has made a false accusation, A must keep the card *and* miss a go.
The object of the game is to collect as few cards as possible. The player with fewest cards at the end is the winner.
There is a rules sheet for this game at the back of the book.

40 The last game

Type of activity
whole class
search

Function practised
thanking

Exponent
Thank you (very much) for —ing
I'd like to thank you for —ing
I'd like to say thank you for —ing, etc.

Lexical areas
classroom activities, character

Essential vocabulary
colourful, even later than, pronounce, laugh, smile, helpful, enthusiastic, cheerful, jokes, thoughtful

How to use the game

This is a game for the end of term (if you have had a class you enjoyed and who got on well). It can be played with any number of students.
Copy one questionnaire for each student and give them out.
Ask the students to find someone to thank for each of the actions on the questionnaire.
The object of the game is to find someone for each of the actions mentioned on the questionnaire.
(In practice everyone gets thanked for something because if someone is thanking you for something, you also instinctively thank them.)
You might prefer to make your own questionnaire, based on your knowledge of the students and class mythology that has built up over the term.

1 TOWER BLOCK (Role cards – ground floor)

You live on the ground floor. You are a biochemistry student and you play a lot of tennis. No one lives on your left, but in the room on the right there is a history student who plays the saxophone, very often and very noisily. Above you there is a chemistry student who is a fitness fanatic and does early morning exercises at 6 a.m. every morning. With all this noise, it's hard to concentrate on your work!

You live on the ground floor. You are a history student, but you're very interested in jazz and you play the saxophone in a jazz band. To your right there are two art students – you don't know much about them. To your left there's a biochemist, sporty type, plays tennis. Above you there's a philosophy student – there's always a group of them there – you can hear their voices droning on and on late at night – you can't think what they find to talk about for so long.

You study art and share a room with another art student. On one side of you there's a student who plays the saxophone and on the other side of you there's a student who plays the violin. *And* above you there's a student with a computer – you can hear the wretched thing bleeping away all night.

You study art and share a room with another art student, on the ground floor.

You are a music student (violin) and live on the ground floor. In the room next door on the left there are two art students and on the other side there's an English literature student who has late night parties nearly every night. Above you there's a biology student who plays the guitar terribly badly. You're very sensitive about music and you can't bear it. You'd like to move!

You are an English lit. student and live on the ground floor. You hate this place! Next to you there's a music student who is always practising the violin and above you there are two students who are always quarrelling. And the other student next door...you haven't said anything, but you're sure there's a cat in there – you can hear it yowling sometimes. It's against college regulations to keep pets.

You study geography and live on the ground floor, in the end room. On your left there's a very noisy English literature student, has parties all the time. And above you there's a physics student. You don't know *what* goes on in that room, but there are the most extraordinary noises coming from it at all hours of the day and night. You don't like to complain though, since you have a secret – although it's against college regulations, you have a pet – a kitten. You don't think anyone knows and you don't want to be found out.

1 TOWER BLOCK (Role cards – first floor)

You're a chemistry student and a fitness freak. You don't know the other students in the college very well, but there's a philosophy student next door – usually a whole bunch of philosophy students actually, up till all hours, working out the meaning of life or whatever. At least there's no one the other side (you have an end room) and above you there's only the warden who's very quiet.

You're a philosophy student and you have a room in between two fanatics. One is a fitness freak and wakes you up at six every morning, bouncing around doing exercises and the other is a computer buff and spends the whole time bleeping away on a stupid machine. As if that weren't enough, the room above you is occupied by someone very strange, judging by the grunts and yells coming from that room. You've never met them, and you wouldn't want to!

You're a computer science student and you have a very noisy room on the first floor. On your right there's a biology student who plays the guitar excruciatingly badly and on the other side there's a philosophy student who has earnest and excitable discussions late at night. You can't think what these philosophy students get so worked up about. And above you there's some kind of amateur jazz musician.

You're a biology student, but spend most of your time learning the guitar. In fact, you'd like to give up biology and study guitar. Your room is very noisy. On the left there's a computer student, spends most of the time playing with a home computer and on the other side there are two French students who spend most of the time quarrelling. Above you there's a fitness fanatic, a PE student who spends the whole time thumping up and down doing aerobic exercises.

You study French and share a room on the first floor with another French student. You wish you didn't as you don't get on well.

You study French and share a room with another French student. You don't get on very well. Next to you on one side there's a guitar player, and on the other there's a physics student. You don't know *what* goes on in that room but there are some extraordinary noises coming from it sometimes. Above you there's an Italian student who's an opera buff...

You study physics and are doing a PhD in sound and vibration research. You have two very noisy neighbours in the room on your left: two very quarrelsome French students – you wish they'd leave each other alone. You have an end room on the first floor so there's no one on your right, but above you there's an architecture student who plays the double bass. Just as well you don't work in your room. Most of your work is done up at the lab, though you do try out the tapes you need for your experiments back in your room occasionally.

1 TOWER BLOCK (Role cards – second floor)

You are the college warden and have an end room on the second floor. It's pretty noisy in this college and you're often having to tell the students to keep the noise down. Above you there are two foreign students from Africa – they play very odd music. And next to you there is an anthropology student – the noises that come from that room are indescribable! You thought there was something very odd going on there until you had a word about it and found out that the noises were tape recordings of grunts and yells of some tribe they're researching in the Anthropology Department.

You study anthropology (you're doing research into the war cries of tribes in the Upper Volta) and you have a rather noisy room in hall. On your right is a medical student who plays jazz very loudly late at night and above you is someone who plays the cello. At least your other neighbour is quite quiet – it's the college warden.

You're a medical student and have a room in college. College! It's more like a zoo! Above you are some very noisy sociology students who have late night discussions and on your right there's a PE student who does early morning exercises. Between them they completely ruin your night's sleep. But the worst is the student next door on the left. You don't know *what* is going on in that room, but you've never heard noises like that in your life...At least your interest (jazz) is harmless.

You're a PE student and have a room on the second floor between a jazz freak and an opera buff. And above you there's someone learning Chinese, practises tones all day long...the place is a lunatic asylum!

You study Italian and love Italian opera. You live on the second floor, between an architecture student who plays the double bass and a PE student who wakes you up at six every morning with noisy exercises. At least there's no one living in the room above you.

You study architecture and play the double bass. You live in quite a musical corner of the college. Next to you, on the left, there's an Italian student who's an opera buff and above you there is a Russian student who likes folk dancing. You wish he/she wouldn't practise it on your ceiling though... You have an end room so there's no one the other side, thank goodness.

1 TOWER BLOCK (Role cards – third floor)

You are a Kenyan student and share an end room on the third floor with another African. Next to you there's a maths student who plays the cello and above you there's an engineer who has wild parties. You don't mind the noise though.

You are a Nigerian student and share with another African student.

You study maths and play the cello. You have a rather noisy room and would like to change it. On your left there are two foreign students who play odd music and cook strange things and on your right there's a sociologist who is forever having noisy discussions. You can't understand why people get so worked up over ideas. Above you there's someone who studies Greek and must be a fitness fanatic judging from the early morning thumps and thuds...

You are a sociologist and live in a room on the third floor between a cello player and someone who's always doing strange voice exercises. At least the room above you is fairly quiet.

You study Chinese and are having a lot of trouble with the pronunciation. You wish you had a quieter room so you could concentrate. On your left there is a sociologist and above you there's a politics student. Both of these spend the whole time arguing and shouting and having endless heated discussions. The walls are so thin you can hear every word – and a lot of nonsense it all is. You're heartily sick of the words 'parameter', 'situation', and 'viable'. At least the room on your right is empty.

You study Russian and are particularly interested in Russian folk culture. You are learning several Russian dances. You have an end room on the third floor, and the room on your left is empty, so it's fairly quiet.

1 TOWER BLOCK (Role cards – fourth floor)

You study mechanical engineering and have the end room on the fourth floor next to someone who studies Greek and wakes you up at six every morning doing aerobic exercises. The two students above you, who study German, are always quarrelling, so it's pretty noisy here.

You study Greek and have a room in college, but you wish you didn't. Your left hand neighbour is a mechanical engineer who has wild parties every night and above you there's a civil engineer who has card parties. Sometimes you can't get to sleep till three or four in the morning and you have to get up at six to do your aerobics and learn your irregular verbs. On the other side there's a nurse who's pretty quiet.

You're doing a nursing degree and are on night duty at the moment. At least most of the people are out during the day so you can get some sleep, but the student above you seems to have a dog: you can hear it barking during the day. It's against the regulations of course, to keep pets. Your other neighbours are a Greek student on your left and a politics student on your right.

You study politics and live on the fourth floor between a nursing student and an education student. Neither of them give you much trouble, but above you there's an agricultural student who gets up at about five every morning, God knows what for, to milk the cows or something probably. You're a late-night person, so object to being woken up so early.

You study education and have a room between a politics student and an oceanographer. The politics student has heated late-night discussions with friends almost every night, keeping you awake till three or four sometimes. Why do politicians always shout so loud? The oceanographer is a harmless chap, but has a budgie (strange pet for an oceanographer) which cheeps and whistles early in the morning. So between the politics and the budgie, you don't get much sleep. The student upstairs plays the drums every afternoon, so no chance of an afternoon nap either...

You study oceanography and have an end room on the fourth floor, next to an education student. Above you there's an economics student who belongs to a morris dancing society and practises the steps, bells and all, right over your head.

1 TOWER BLOCK (Role cards – fifth floor)

You study German and share a room on the fifth floor with another German student. Pity you don't get on...

You study German and share with another German student. You quarrel a lot. You have an end room, but your neighbour on the right, an engineering student, is very fond of cards and has card parties most evenings. There's an engineering student below you too, who also has noisy late night parties. And above you there's a Spanish student with a parrot. Worse than an alarm clock, that parrot, wakes you up at half past five every morning by swearing in Spanish.

You are a civil engineer and have a room between two bickering German students and an Arabic student with a noisy dog. It's against the rules to keep pets. You're surprised the warden hasn't found out about it – it's always yapping. But your worst neighbour is the one above you. You play cards till late most nights, so you like to lie in, but the student above you does early morning exercises, and thumps around on the floor for about an hour between six and seven every day.

You study classical Arabic and have a room between a civil engineer, on the left, who has noisy late night parties and an agriculture student, on the right, who gets up at half past five every day. The student above you has late night parties too. You never get any sleep. But you don't like to complain because they might protest about your dog. It's strictly against the rules to keep pets in the college and you don't want the warden to find out.

You study agriculture and have a very noisy room on the fifth floor between a student who plays the drums and a student with a yappy dog. You like to get up early and the student upstairs has a baby which cries at night and keeps you awake so you never get enough sleep. You know pets aren't allowed in the college, surely babies aren't either.

You study electrical engineering and play the drums in a local rock group. You have a room between an agricultural student and an economics student. Neither give you much trouble – anyway you're usually too busy practising drums to hear anything. There are two accountancy students upstairs, but they're very quiet.

You study economics and have an end room on the fifth floor. Your next door neighbour is an engineer who plays the drums very loudly in the afternoons – just when you want to put some folk music on and practise your morris dancing steps. Upstairs are some very noisy drama students.

1 TOWER BLOCK (Role cards – sixth floor)

You study Spanish and have an end room on the top floor which you share with your parrot. You're very proud of Pedro because you've taught him to swear in Spanish – he has a perfect accent. You like your room, the only problem is the food technologist next door who leaps around doing exercises at some unearthly hour in the morning and of course wakes the parrot who starts swearing in Spanish...

You study food technology and have a room between a Spanish student and a pharmacist. The Spanish student has a rather rude parrot, but that's no problem compared to the pharmacist's late night parties. You like to get up early in the morning to do your fitness training, so resent being kept awake late at night...

You study pharmacy and have a room on the top floor between a food technology student (on the left) and a geologist (on the right). Neither are ideal neighbours – you go to bed late so you like to lie in in the mornings, but the food technologist gets up at about five and crashes around doing exercises, and the geologist has a baby which yells and screams all night and early in the morning. You've had a word with them, but all they do is moan about your parties.

You study geology and are having a hard time since you have a six month old baby. She shouldn't be in college with you, but what else can you do? Just hope the warden doesn't find out. Your right hand neighbours are two very quiet accountants but your left hand neighbour is a pharmacist who has noisy late night parties that keep the baby – and you awake.

You are an accountant and share a room on the top floor with another accountancy student.

You study accountancy and share a room with another accountant. You have noisy neighbours – a student with a screaming baby, on the left, and a group of hysterical drama students, on the right. You're fed up.

You are a drama student and have sixn end room on the top floor next to a pair of dozy accountants. It's so quiet in there you reckon they've probably sent each other to sleep! You're working hard on a play at the moment and a group of you often have rehearsals in your room.

1 TOWER BLOCK (Floor plan)

SIXTH FLOOR

| Spanish student | Food technology student | Pharmacy student | Geology student | Two accountancy students | Drama student |

FIFTH FLOOR

| Two German students | Civil engineering student | Classical Arabic student | Agricultural student | Electrical engineering student | Economics student |

FOURTH FLOOR

| Mechanical engineering student | Greek student | Student nurse | Politics student | Education student | Oceanography student |

THIRD FLOOR

| Two African students | Maths student | Sociology student | Chinese student | (empty) | Russian student |

SECOND FLOOR

| College warden | Anthropology student | Medical student | P.E. student | Italian student | Architecture student |

FIRST FLOOR

| Chemistry student | Philosophy student | Computer science student | Biology student | Two French students | Physics student |

GROUND FLOOR

| Biochemistry student | History student | Two art students | Music student | English literature student | Geography student |

2 WHATSITSNAME?

2 WHATSITSNAME?

3 THE THREE WISHES GAME (Granting cards)

You have the power to grant any wishes to do with

LOVE

You have the power to grant any wishes to do with

MONEY

You have the power to grant any wishes to do with

WORK

You have the power to grant any wishes to do with

TALENTS AND ABILITIES

You have the power to grant any wishes to do with

POSSESSIONS

You have the power to grant any wishes to do with

TRAVEL

You have the power to grant any wishes to do with

TIME

You have the power to grant any wishes to do with

APPEARANCE

You have the power to grant any wishes to do with

PERSONALITY

You have the power to grant any wishes to do with

FAME

4 RELATIVELY SPEAKING

5 LIFESWAP

5 LIFESWAP

6 MATCHMAKING

Name ....
Age ....
Job ....

Likes ....
Dislikes ....
Hobbies ....

Name ....
Age ....
Job ....

Likes ....
Dislikes ....
Hobbies ....

Name ....
Age ....
Job ....

Likes ....
Dislikes ....
Hobbies ....

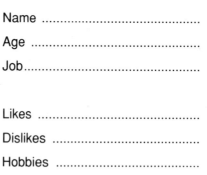

Name ....
Age ....
Job ....

Likes ....
Dislikes ....
Hobbies ....

Name ....
Age ....
Job ....

Likes ....
Dislikes ....
Hobbies ....

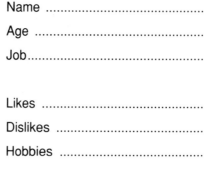

Name ....
Age ....
Job ....

Likes ....
Dislikes ....
Hobbies ....

Name ....
Age ....
Job ....

Likes ....
Dislikes ....
Hobbies ....

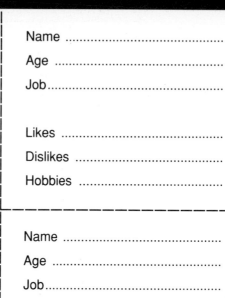

Name ....
Age ....
Job ....

Likes ....
Dislikes ....
Hobbies ....

Name ....
Age ....
Job ....

Likes ....
Dislikes ....
Hobbies ....

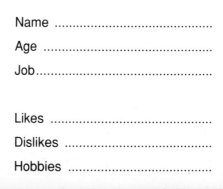

Name ....
Age ....
Job ....

Likes ....
Dislikes ....
Hobbies ....

6 MATCHMAKING

Name ....
Age ....
Job ....

Likes ....
Dislikes ....
Hobbies ....

Name ....
Age ....
Job ....

Likes ....
Dislikes ....
Hobbies ....

Name ....
Age ....
Job ....

Likes ....
Dislikes ....
Hobbies ....

Name ....
Age ....
Job ....

Likes ....
Dislikes ....
Hobbies ....

Name ....
Age ....
Job ....

Likes ....
Dislikes ....
Hobbies ....

Name ....
Age ....
Job ....

Likes ....
Dislikes ....
Hobbies ....

Name ....
Age ....
Job ....

Likes ....
Dislikes ....
Hobbies ....

Name ....
Age ....
Job ....

Likes ....
Dislikes ....
Hobbies ....

Name ....
Age ....
Job ....

Likes ....
Dislikes ....
Hobbies ....

Name ....
Age ....
Job ....

Likes ....
Dislikes ....
Hobbies ....

7 WHOSE? (Questionnaire)

1 ....is a student whose mother ...

2 ....is a student whose father ...

3 ....is a student whose brother ...

4 ....is a student whose sister ...

5 ....is a student whose favourite book is ...

6 ....is a student whose hobby is ...

7 ....is a student whose dog is called ...

8 ....is a student whose ambition is to ...

9 ....is a student whose pet hate is ...

10 ....is a student whose hero/heroine is ...

---

1 ....is a student whose mother ...

2 ....is a student whose father ...

3 ....is a student whose brother ...

4 ....is a student whose sister ...

5 ....is a student whose favourite book is ...

6 ....is a student whose hobby is ...

7 ....is a student whose dog is called ...

8 ....is a student whose ambition is to ...

9 ....is a student whose pet hate is ...

10 ....is a student whose hero/heroine is ...

---

1 ....is a student whose mother ...

2 ....is a student whose father ...

3 ....is a student whose brother ...

4 ....is a student whose sister ...

5 ....is a student whose favourite book is ...

6 ....is a student whose hobby is ...

7 ....is a student whose dog is called ...

8 ....is a student whose ambition is to ...

9 ....is a student whose pet hate is ...

10 ....is a student whose hero/heroine is ...

---

1 ....is a student whose mother ...

2 ....is a student whose father ...

3 ....is a student whose brother ...

4 ....is a student whose sister ...

5 ....is a student whose favourite book is ...

6 ....is a student whose hobby is ...

7 ....is a student whose dog is called ...

8 ....is a student whose ambition is to ...

9 ....is a student whose pet hate is ...

10 ....is a student whose hero/heroine is ...

8 ALIEN (Role cards)

You were washing up when you saw a red light in the sky behind the trees at the bottom of the garden. It was moving and flashing on and off.

You were in the field, taking the dog for a walk, when suddenly he became very frightened and started whimpering. You heard a humming noise and suddenly the sky was filled with red light.

You were gardening in the back garden when a saucer-shaped object flew over your head. It seemed to come in to land in the garden of the house at the end of the road. You were so shocked you didn't know what to do.

It was nine o'clock in the morning. You know because you were listening to the news. You heard a humming noise and the whole house shook. You ran out into the garden to see what was happening and saw a large saucer-shaped object flying low overhead. You ran back indoors to telephone the police.

8 ALIEN (Role cards)

You were washing up in the kitchen when you heard a loud humming noise and the air was full of a red light. You ran outside and saw the large saucer-shaped spaceship had landed in your back garden. Three things were getting out. They had six arms and three heads and wore a kind of uniform. One of them saw you and pointed a gun at you. There was a flash. You fell down, and when you woke up, the spaceship had gone. Perhaps it was a dream.

You saw everything from an upstairs window. You were cleaning your bedroom windows when you heard a loud humming noise and a saucer-shaped object came whizzing past the window. It landed in the next-door garden. Three men got out. They had six arms and three heads and were dressed in uniform. Your neighbour came running out of his house and one of the men pointed a gun at him and shot him. Two men went into the house and one stayed by the spaceship. He wandered round the garden, smelling the flowers. He picked an apple off the tree and took a bite, but spat it out at once. Then he picked a bunch of roses. The other men came back and they all got into the spaceship. The third man was still carrying the roses. Maybe they were for his wife.

You were upstairs playing a game called *Alien Invader* on your home computer when suddenly two strange men came into the house. They had three heads and six arms. You were at a very exciting part of the game: you had just fired a rocket to destroy a spaceship, but one of the men picked you up and held you fast while the other sat down at your computer. He typed in some commands at the keyboard. Then the other man released you and they both left. When you looked at your computer screen you found that your rocket attack had been diverted.

You are a policeman. You were driving along your usual route in your police car when a call over the radio told you to go to Western Road where some madwoman thought she had seen a UFO.

8 ALIEN (Role cards)

You came home from doing the shopping to find your husband in a state of panic. He says that a UFO landed in your back garden and that an alien shot him. Your son says that two aliens came into the bedroom and interfered with his computer game. You think they're teasing you.

You were playing in your bedroom, when your brother came in shouting something about UFO's and rocket attacks and his computer game. You think it's all silly – he's obsessed with science-fiction and computer games.

You were hanging out the washing, when you saw a red light in the sky behind the trees at the bottom of the garden. It was moving and flashing on and off.

You were out for a morning walk. You heard a humming noise and suddenly the sky was filled with red light.

8 ALIEN (Role cards)

You were in the back garden when a saucer-shaped object flew over your head. It seemed to come in to land in the garden of the house at the end of the road. You were so shocked you didn't know what to do.

It was nine o'clock in the morning. You know because you were listening to the news. You heard a humming noise, and the whole house shook. You ran out into the garden to see what was happening and saw a large saucer-shaped object flying low overhead. Now you don't know whether you dreamt it or not.

You were having breakfast in the back garden when a saucer-shaped object flew over your head. It seemed to come in to land in the garden of the house at the end of the road. You were so shocked you didn't know what to do.

You heard a humming noise, and the whole house shook. You ran out into the garden to see what was happening and saw a large saucer-shaped object flying low overhead. You ran back indoors to telephone the fire brigade.

8 ALIEN (Questionnaire)

Correct the mistakes in the pictures and put them in the right order.

Write the first letter of each answer in the box. Then rearrange the letters to find where the aliens came from.

What colour were the spaceship's lights? ☐

How many heads did the aliens have? ☐

What were they wearing? ☐

What shape was the spaceship? ☐

What fruit did the alien pick in the garden? ☐

What time was it? ☐

The aliens came from ....

9 SCI-FI DOMINOES

9 FAIRYTALE DOMINOES

10 CROSSED LINES (Task sheets)

---

1. Phone the Gaumont Theatre and find out what play is on this week. Is there a matinee on Saturday?
2. Phone the station and find out the times of trains to Bristol on a weekday morning.
3. Phone the dentist and make an appointment for Wednesday afternoon.
4. Phone the doctor and make an appointment for Friday.
5. Phone the Odeon Cinema and ask what time the film *Roger Rabbit III* begins?

---

1. Phone the Gaumont Theatre and find out what play is on next week.
2. Phone the station and find out the times of trains to Oxford on a Sunday morning.
3. Phone the dentist and make an appointment for Friday afternoon.
4. Phone the doctor and make an appointment for this week sometime.
5. Phone the Odeon Cinema and ask what time the last performance of the film *Roger Rabbit III* ends?

---

1. Phone the Gaumont Theatre and book two tickets for *Hamlet* on Friday or Saturday.
2. Phone the station and find out the times of the first train to London on Sunday.
3. Phone the dentist and make an appointment for Thursday afternoon.
4. Phone the doctor and make an appointment for one afternoon this week.
5. Phone the Odeon Cinema and ask what's on this week.

---

1. Phone the Gaumont Theatre and find out what play is on this week. Are there any tickets left for Saturday night?
2. Phone the station and find out the times of trains to Birmingham.
3. Phone the dentist and make an appointment. Any time this week will do.
4. Phone the doctor and make an appointment for this week.
5. Phone the Odeon Cinema and ask if you can book tickets for the film *Roger Rabbit III*.

---

1. Phone the Gaumont Theatre and find out how long *Hamlet* is on for. You need four tickets, early next week if possible.
2. Phone the station and find out the times of trains to Gatwick airport. You need to be there by 10 a.m. next Thursday.
3. Phone the dentist and make an appointment for as soon as possible.
4. Phone the doctor and make an appointment for as soon as possible.
5. Phone the Odeon Cinema and ask if there is a matinee performance of the film *Roger Rabbit III*.

10 CROSSED LINES (Information sheets)

GAUMONT THEATRE

This week until Friday: *HAMLET*

Every night 7.30 p.m.
Matinee Saturday 2 p.m.
Performance ends 11.30 p.m.
Tickets: £10 £12 £15
Tickets at all prices available every evening

Next week for four weeks:
CHARLIE'S AUNT: a comedy

STATION

Trains to:
Bristol weekdays: 7 a.m. 9 a.m. 11a.m.
1 p.m. 3 p.m. 5 p.m 7 p.m. 9 p.m. 11 p.m.
Sundays: 9 a.m. 1 p.m. 5 p.m. 9 p.m.
Oxford weekdays: every hour from 6.10 a.m. to 12.10 a.m.
Sundays: every hour from 6.10 a.m. to 12.10 a.m.
Birmingham weekdays: 7.30 a.m.
10.15 a.m. 3.35 p.m. 5.20 p.m. 8.54 p.m.
Sundays: 10.34 a.m. 4.45 p.m. 7.54 p.m.
Gatwick airport every day: every half hour all through the day and night on the hour and half hour
London every day: at twenty past the hour beginning 6.20 a.m., last train 2.20 a.m.

ODEON CINEMA

This week: *ROGER RABBIT III*

Performances 3 p.m. 5 p.m. 7 p.m. 9 p.m.
(last performance ends 11 p.m.)
All tickets £5
Not bookable in advance

DENTIST

	MONDAY	TUESDAY	WEDNESDAY	THURSDAY	FRIDAY
9.00	Mr Privett	Ms Burke			Mr Green
9.30	Mr Green		Mr Craig	Mr Burke	Mr Privett
10.00		Mr Pidduck	Ms Brown		Mr Craig
10.30	Mr Craig		Ms Michel	Mr Pidduck	
11.00	Ms Brown	Mr Beahan		Ms Cunningham	Ms Brown
11.30	Mrs Michel		Mr Tuttle	Mr Beahan	Mrs Michel
12.00			Mrs Laney	Mr Mills	Mr Banks
2.00	Ms Banks	Ms Cunningham		Mr Anderson	Mr Ramsay
2.30	Mr Ramsay	Mrs Laney	Mr Ramsay	Mrs Roodt	Mr Tuttle
3.00	Mr Tuttle	Mr Mills		Mr Craig	
3.30		Mr Anderson	Mr Privett	Ms Hall	
4.00	Ms Hall	Ms Hall	Mr Green		Ms Hall
4.30		Mrs Roodt	Ms Banks		Mrs Laney

DOCTOR

	MONDAY	TUESDAY	WEDNESDAY	THURSDAY	FRIDAY
9.00	Mr Privett	Ms Burke	Mr Craig	Mr Burke	
9.30	Mr Green	Mr Pidduck	Mrs Brown	Mr Pidduck	Mr Green
10.00	Mr Craig	Mr Beahan	Ms Michel	Mrs Cunningham	Mr Privett
10.30	Ms Brown	Ms Cunningham	Mr Tuttle	Mr Beahan	Ms Craig
11.00	Mrs Michel	Ms Laney		Mr Mills	Ms Brown
11.30	Ms Banks	Mr Mills	Ms Laney	Mr Anderson	Mr Michel
12.00		Mr Anderson	Mr Ramsay	Mrs Roodt	Ms Banks
2.00			Mr Privett		Mr Ramsay
2.30	Mr Ramsay		Mr Green		Mr Tuttle
3.00		Mrs Hall	Ms Banks		
3.30	Mr Tuttle	Mrs Roodt			
4.00	Ms Hall			Mr Craig	
4.30				Ms Hall	Mrs Laney

11 IDEAL HOMES (Estate agents signs)

Fold

Sellit and Runne

Fold

Diddle and Cheete

Fold

Fiddle and Grabbe

11 IDEAL HOMES (House cards 1 – 5)

1 Delightful 4 bedroom 18th century house with wealth of intriguing features, secret passages, trapdoors, secret cupboards, etc.

2 Rubber floors, booby traps and distorting mirrors make this 3 bedroom cottage an amusing buy.

3 Set in the grounds of a safari park, this comfortable country house offers the possibility of a home plus income. The garage and conservatory have been skilfully converted to provide luxurious animal cages.

4 Although in need of some repair, this property offers a regal home for the do-it-yourself fanatic.

5 A full-size heated swimming pool with sauna is the outstanding feature of this comfortable family house.

11 IDEAL HOMES (House cards 6 – 10)

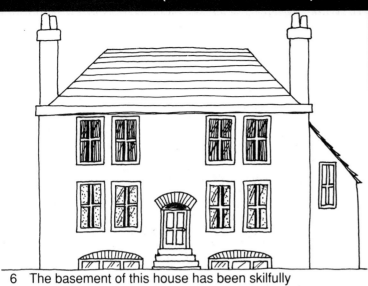

6 The basement of this house has been skilfully converted to form a private cinema with full-size screen and seating for 50.

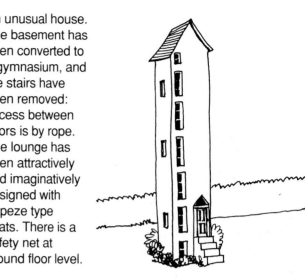

7 An unusual house. The basement has been converted to a gymnasium, and the stairs have been removed: access between floors is by rope. The lounge has been attractively and imaginatively designed with trapeze type seats. There is a safety net at ground floor level.

8 This lovely riverside house has the unusual feature of a large aviary in the garden.

9 The extensive flower and vegetable gardens surrounding this house offer endless possibilities for the keen gardener.

10 This twelve bedroom house is ideal as a guest house or for the larger family.

11 IDEAL HOMES (House cards 11 – 16)

11 Delightful town residence with garden. Accommodation comprises kitchen, dining room, lounge, 3 bedrooms, bathroom.

12 Delightful town residence with garden. Accommodation comprises kitchen, dining room, lounge, 3 bedrooms, bathroom.

13 Delightful town residence with garden. Accommodation comprises kitchen, dining room, lounge, 4 bedrooms, bathroom.

14 Delightful country residence with garden. Accommodation comprises kitchen, dining room, lounge, 3 bedrooms, bathroom.

16 Delightful country residence with garden. Accommodation comprises kitchen, dining room, lounge, 4 bedrooms, bathroom.

15 Delightful country residence with garden. Accommodation comprises kitchen, dining room, lounge, 4 bedrooms, bathroom.

13 GOOD INTENTIONS or THE ROAD TO HELL

Next year I'm going to:
- give up smoking
- give up drinking
- give up eating chocolate
- work harder
- work less
- be a nicer person
- stop shouting at my mum/dad/husband/wife/girlfriend/ boyfriend/ sister/brother
- lose weight
- decorate the house
- be tidier
- do more exercise
- travel more
- read more
- read more
- be more punctual
- watch less TV
- be more decisive
- be more relaxed

and I'm going to ....

Next year I'm going to:
- give up smoking
- give up drinking
- give up eating chocolate
- work harder
- work less
- be a nicer person
- stop shouting at my mum/dad/husband/wife/girlfriend/ boyfriend/ sister/brother
- lose weight
- decorate the house
- be tidier
- do more exercise
- travel more
- read more
- read more
- be more punctual
- watch less TV
- be more decisive
- be more relaxed

and I'm going to ....

14 FUTURE SNAP

By this time tomorrow...	...I'll have finished the book.
Tomorrow evening...	...I'm going to the cinema.
On Friday...	...I'm going to a party.
Next year...	...I'm going to visit my sister in America.
This time next week...	...I'll be in Bangkok.
In the year 2000...	...I'll be 35.
By the time I'm 40...	...I'll have made a lot of money.
When I see him again...	...I'll tell him what I think of him.
After lunch...	...I think I'll go for a walk.

14 FUTURE SNAP

By the time I'm 50...	...I'll be ready to retire.

14 FUTURE SNAP

As soon as I arrive...	...I'll telephone you.
By the time you get this letter...	...I'll have left the country.
At 6 o'clock...	...I'm meeting Jack.
By this time next year...	...I'll have finished my studies.
In 6 months' time...	...I'll be in Australia.
By the end of June...	...I'll have saved £5,000.
When I next see you...	...I'll have started the new job.
This time tomorrow...	...I'll be flying over the Atlantic.
Next week...	...I'm going to get my hair cut.
When he comes back...	...I'll be very happy.

15 TOLD YOU SO! (Now / One year later cards)

NOW	ONE YEAR LATER
Janet in the typing pool has just got engaged. She's only known him a week and they plan to get married next month. They've got nothing in common. You're sure she's making a terrible mistake.	Janet got married, but she's terribly unhappy.
The boss's kid, Tim, is a little devil: always breaking things and being rude. He plays truant from school too – you've seen him.	Tim got expelled from school.
Bob in the accounts department always gets to work late. Yesterday he was nearly an hour late. You know the boss is annoyed about it.	Bob got the sack.
Sam in marketing is engaged but you know his fiancée is still seeing her old boyfriend. You don't know what to do about it.	Sam's fiancee left him and married her boyfriend.
Your colleague, Tony, drinks too much. You're afraid something awful will happen.	Tony had a car crash. He's given up drink.
Your colleagues, Sue and Simon, seem to be spending a lot of money lately on improvements to the house, a new car, new clothes... You know they're not that rich, so they must be getting themselves in debt.	Simon went bankrupt. They had to sell the house.
Your colleague Tessa is always rowing with her husband. She often looks unhappy, and yesterday you saw her crying.	Tessa got divorced.
Mike, in sales, has a teenage son called Billy. Billy is a nice kid, but he has a really rough lot of friends. You're sure they'll get him into trouble. In fact you saw the police come round to his house yesterday.	Billy got a two year prison sentence for shop-lifting.

15 TOLD YOU SO! (Questionnaire)

How much do you know about these people's problems?

What do you think they should do?

1 Janet and her new boyfriend.
2 The boss's son, Tim.
3 Bob in the accounts department.
4 Sam's fiancée and the old boyfriend.
5 Tony.
6 Sue and Simon and their new car.
7 Tessa and her husband.
8 Billy and his gang of friends.

What do you think will probably happen?

Write a prediction for each.

1 Janet will probably ....

2 Tim will probably ....

3 Bob will probably ....

4 Sam's fiancee will probably ....

5 Tony will probably ....

6 Sue and Simon will probably ....

7 Tessa will probably ....

8 Billy will probably ....

16 WHY NOT?

If everyone suddenly went colour blind...

If everyone forgot how to read...

If we could all read each others' thoughts...

If everyone had eyes in the back of their heads...

If stones were used as money...

If animals could speak...

If cars ran on milk...

If people forgot how to talk...

If there was no daylight...

If people were five metres tall...

If broadcasting and printing were banned...

If people lived forever...

17 OFFICE POLITICS

JO
Someone in your department is going to be promoted to supervisor. Naturally, you hope it's going to be you.
You wouldn't mind if Sam or Alex gets the job. Sam's very efficient and Alex is a nice cheerful person. But you hope it's not Terry or Pip. Terry's very bad-tempered and Pip's hopeless at figures.

Talk to people and find out what they think. Try to convince them of your opinion. Don't tell anyone directly what you think of them, of course, but you can tell them what other people think of them, if you like. Your main aim, though, is to find out what other people think about you!

SAM
Someone in your department is going to be promoted to supervisor. Naturally, you hope it's going to be you.
You wouldn't mind if Alex or Terry gets the job. Alex is a cheerful sort of person and Terry is good-natured. But you hope it's not going to be Pip or Robin! Pip is absolutely hopeless at figures and Robin is so rigid and narrow-minded.

Talk to people and find out what they think. Try to convince them of your opinion. Don't tell anyone directly what you think of them, of course, but you can tell them what other people think of them, if you like. Your main aim, though, is to find out what other people think about you!

ALEX
Someone in your department is going to be promoted to supervisor. Naturally, you hope it's going to be you.
You wouldn't mind if Terry or Pip gets the job. Terry is very good-natured and kind and Pip is very careful and precise: very good with figures. But it would be a disaster to have Robin or Jan. Robin is so narrow-minded and Jan is so careless and disorganised.

Talk to people and find out what they think. Try to convince them of your opinion. Don't tell anyone directly what you think of them, of course, but you can tell them what other people think about them, if you like. Your main aim, though, is to find out what other people think about you!

TERRY
Someone in your department is going to be promoted to supervisor. Naturally, you hope it's going to be you.
You wouldn't mind if Pip or Robin gets the job. Pip is very careful and precise: very good with the accounts and Robin is very flexible and open-minded. But it would be terrible if Jan or Chris got the job! Jan is totally disorganised and Chris is so pompous.

Talk to people and find out what they think. Try to convince them of your opinion. Don't tell anyone directly what you think of them, of course, but you can tell them what other people think about them, if you like. Your main aim, though, is to find out what other people think about you!

17 OFFICE POLITICS

PIP
Someone in your department is going to be promoted to supervisor. Naturally, you hope it's going to be you.
You wouldn't mind if Robin or Jan gets the job. Robin is a very tolerant and flexible person and Jan is very organised. But you'd hate to have to work for Chris or Jo! Chris is so unbelievably pompous and Jo is so indecisive.

Talk to people and find out what they think. Try to convince them of your opinion. Don't tell anyone directly what you think of them, of course, but you can tell them what other people think about them, if you like. Your main aim, though, is to find out what other people think about you!

ROBIN
Someone in your department is going to be promoted to supervisor. Naturally, you hope it's going to be you.
You wouldn't mind if Jan or Chris gets the job. Jan is very competent and organised and Chris is a nice, unpretentious down-to-earth sort of person. But it would be a disaster if Jo or Sam got the job. Jo is so weak and indecisive and Sam is very inefficient.

Talk to people and find out what they think. Try to convince them of your opinion. Don't tell anyone directly what you think of them, of course, but you can tell them what other people think about them, if you like. Your main aim, though, is to find out what other people think about you!

JAN
Someone in your department is going to be promoted to supervisor. Naturally, you hope it's going to be you.
You wouldn't mind if it's Chris or Jo. Chris is a very pleasant, down-to-earth person and Jo is a good decision-maker. But it would be dreadful if Sam or Alex were promoted! Sam is terribly inefficient and Alex is a grumpy, miserable sort of character: always moaning and complaining.

Talk to people and find out what they think. Try to convince them of your opinion. Don't tell anyone directly what you think of them, of course, but you can tell them what other people think about them, if you like. Your main aim, though, is to find out what other people think about you!

CHRIS
Someone in your department is going to be promoted to supervisor. Naturally, you hope it's going to be you.
You wouldn't mind if Jo or Sam gets the job. Jo thinks clearly and is decisive, and Sam is a very efficient worker. But it would be awful to have Alex or Terry in charge! Alex is always so grumpy and Terry has a terrible temper.

Talk to people and find out what they think. Try to convince them of your opinion. Don't tell anyone directly what you think of them, of course, but you can tell them what other people think about them, if you like. Your main aim, though, is to find out what other people think about you!

17 OFFICE POLITICS

GERRY
You've just joined the firm and you don't know many of the people yet. However, you don't like Jo much – seems a rather weak and indecisive person. Sam seems more efficient.

TONI
You've just joined the firm and you don't know many of the people yet. However, you don't like Sam much – seems very inefficient. Alex seems nice and cheerful, always making jokes. Gerry joined at the same time as you: very nice, but rather shy.

LESLIE
You've just joined the firm and don't know many of the people yet. However, you don't like Alex, who seems a miserable type: told you off for being late. Terry seems nicer: very good-natured and kind-hearted – showed you how the coffee machine worked on your first day. Toni joined at the same time as you: very nice but a bit forgetful.

DANI
You've just joined the firm and don't know many of the people yet. However, you don't like Terry, who is very bad-tempered and shouted at you on your first day. Pip seems nicer: much more gentle. Leslie joined at the same time as you: very nice but a bit moody.

17 OFFICE POLITICS

PHIL
You've just joined the firm and you don't know many of the people yet. However, you don't like Pip much – seems to be very muddled and added up your wages wrong. Robin seems nice, very tolerant and broad-minded. Dani joined at the same time as you: very nice, but a bit absent minded.

BOBBIE
You've just joined the firm and you don't know many of the people yet. However, you don't like Robin much: a very narrow-minded and inflexible character. Jan, who showed you round on your first day seems very organised. Phil joined at the same time as you: very nice but not very punctual.

PADDY
You've just joined the firm and you don't know many of the people yet. However, you don't like Jan much – seems very disorganised to you. Chris was very friendly to you on your first day: very natural and not a bit standoffish. Bobbie joined at the same time as you: very nice but rather vague.

SANDY
You've just joined the firm and you don't know many of the people yet. However, you don't like Chris much – seems rather cold and pompous and was very rude to you on your first day. Jo would make a good supervisor: firm and decisive. Paddy joined at the same time as you: very nice but a bit eccentric.

18 YUCK!

19 SALES REPS

The Scrub'n'sweep Homecare Machine

The Cordonbleu Haute Cuisine Machine

The Sleepyhead Wake-up Machine

The Hamlet Decision-maker

The Lazibones Keep-fit Machine

The Lexicon English Facilitator

20 PARENT POWER

When you were a child:

were you sent to bed at a certain time?

were you allowed to watch as much TV as you liked?

were you made to do your homework every night?

were you allowed to eat as many sweets as you liked?

were you bought a lot of toys?

were you ever smacked?

When you were a teenager:

were you allowed to wear what you wanted?

were you given a certain time to be in at night?

were you allowed to go out as often as you wanted?

were you allowed to have parties at home?

were you given a large amount of pocket money?

were you made to help with the housework?

YES	NO

When you were a child:

were you sent to bed at a certain time?

were you allowed to watch as much TV as you liked?

were you made to do your homework every night?

were you allowed to eat as many sweets as you liked?

were you bought a lot of toys?

were you ever smacked?

When you were a teenager:

were you allowed to wear what you wanted?

were you given a certain time to be in at night?

were you allowed to go out as often as you wanted?

were you allowed to have parties at home?

were you given a large amount of pocket money?

were you made to help with the housework?

YES	NO

21 PROMISES, PROMISES

MUM
You want Lucy to promise to be home by 11 o'clock on Saturday.
You want Tom to promise never to ride a motorbike.
You want Dad to promise to paint the kitchen.
You want someone to help you with the ironing.

DAD
You want Mum to promise to invite some important people (the Jones) to dinner – she can't stand them.
You want Grandpa to promise to take Grandma on holiday.
You want Grandma to promise to stop moaning about never going on holiday.
You want someone to pick you up from the station on Monday night at 11.30.

TOM
You want Mum to promise to lend you the car on Saturday night.
You want Lucy to lend you £5.
You want Grandpa to promise to help you with your homework.
You want someone to promise to buy you a guitar for your birthday.

LUCY
You want Mum to promise to let you go to the party on Saturday night.
You want Grandma to lend you £10.
You want Tom to promise to give you a lift to the party.
You want someone to promise to buy you a bicycle next birthday.

GRANDPA
You want Dad to promise to mend the fence.
You want Tom to promise to mow the lawn this weekend.
You want Grandma to mend your shirts (she hates sewing).
You want someone to promise to chop the wood.

GRANDMA
You want Lucy to promise to help with the housework.
You want Grandpa to promise to go away on holiday this summer.
You want Dad to look after the cat if you go away.
You want someone to weed the garden.

AUNTIE JOAN
You want someone to promise to clear the attic for you.
You want someone to paint the garden gate.
You want someone to promise to do the shopping for you next Saturday.
You want someone to promise to pick you up at the airport next Sunday.

SUSIE
You want someone to take you to the party on Wednesday.
You want someone to promise to take you to next week's film at the Ritz.
You want someone to lend you £5.
You want someone to promise to buy you a stereo for your next birthday.

22 IT WASN'T ME, OFFICER (Thief cards)

You are a thief. You specialise in jewellers' shops. Last week you did a big jeweller's in Paris and got away with £50,000. Don't let anyone know you've been to Paris, though it's safe to mention other countries. Portugal for example – you went there two weeks ago, but that was for pleasure, not work. Talk about your hobbies: opera, old cars...

You are an art thief. Last week you stole two paintings from a museum in Amsterdam. Don't let anyone know you've been to Holland, or know anything about art. Talk about your interests: jazz, travel – you've been on the Trans-Siberian railway and you've seen the Pyramids.

You are a bank robber. Last week you did a bank in South London and got away with £60,000. Don't let anyone know you were in London last week. Tell them you went to Madrid to see the match against Real Madrid – that's true as it happens, but you did the robbery when you got back!

You are a burglar. Last week you got into a house in New York, and got away with a quarter of a million pounds' worth of antiques. Don't let anyone know you've ever been to New York. You can talk about other places you've visited: Greece, Turkey, but not the States. Or you can talk about your interests: you love animals – you used to keep a lion cub and a koala bear, but you had to sell them, because your work involves so much travel.

You are a gold smuggler. Last week you brought £300,000 worth of gold from Hong Kong into Britain. Be careful! Don't let anyone know you've ever been to Hong Kong (although you go there once a month on 'business'). Talk about other places you've been – Japan, Thailand – if you like, or about your hobby: bird watching.

You are a car thief. Last week you were in Rome where you stole 6 Alfa Romeos, 5 Lamborghinis and 10 Ferraris. But be careful! Don't let anyone know you've been to Italy, although you go there quite often on 'business' (you're crazy about Italian cars). Talk about other countries you've been to – Switzerland, Norway – or about your hobbies – skiing and mountain walking.

22 IT WASN'T ME, OFFICER (Police cards)

You are a police officer and you are looking for a jewellery thief. Don't let anyone know this though! The person you are looking for robbed a jewellery shop in Paris last week and stole £50,000 of jewellery. They found some clues at the scene of the crime: a wallet containing an opera ticket, some Portuguese stamps and an entrance ticket to the Transport Museum in London. Talk to people about their hobbies and travels, and see if you can find anyone who could be the thief. If you do suspect someone, don't say anything, act naturally and wait till the end of the game.

You are a police officer, and you are looking for an art thief. Don't let anyone know this though! The person you are looking for robbed an art gallery in Amsterdam last week and stole two paintings. They found some clues at the scene of the crime: a wallet containing a ticket to a jazz concert, a postcard of the Pyramids and an old ticket from the Trans-Siberian railway. Talk to people about their hobbies and travels, and see if you can find anyone who could be the thief. If you do suspect someone, don't say anything, act naturally and wait till the end of the game.

You are a police officer, and you are looking for a bank robber. Don't let anyone know this though! The person you are looking for robbed a bank in London last week and stole £60,000. There was a clue at the scene of the crime: the robber dropped an old airline ticket to Madrid and a ticket stub from a football match there. Talk to people about their hobbies and travels, and see if you can find anyone who could be the thief. If you do suspect someone, don't say anything, act naturally and wait till the end of the game.

You are a police officer, and you are looking for a burglar – a very successful one. Don't let anyone know this though! The person you are looking for burgled a house in New York last week and stole £250,000 of antiques. They found some clues at the scene of the crime: the burglar had dropped a wallet containing some Greek and Turkish money and some photos of a lion cub and a koala bear. Talk to people about their hobbies and travels, and see if you can find anyone who could be the thief. If you do suspect someone, don't say anything, act naturally and wait till the end of the game.

You are a police officer, and you are looking for a gold smuggler. Don't let anyone know this though! The person you are looking for smuggled £300,000 worth of gold from Hong Kong to London last week. There are some clues though: a bag containing an incriminating letter, a guide book to Japan and a book on bird-watching were found on the plane. Talk to people about their hobbies and travels, and see if you can find anyone who could be the thief. If you do suspect someone, don't say anything, act naturally and wait till the end of the game.

You are a police officer, and you are looking for a car thief. Don't let anyone know this though! The person you are looking for stole a large number of Italian cars in Rome last week. There are some clues though: one of the stolen Alfa Romeos was found and in the boot were a Swiss ski pass, a pair of walking boots and a guide to Norway. Talk to people about their hobbies and travels, and see if you can find anyone who could be the thief. If you do suspect someone, don't say anything, act naturally and wait till the end of the game.

23 GUESS WHAT I'VE BEEN DOING!

24 SCHOOL REUNION (Role cards)

ALEX
You are a successful actor.

You're very curious about what has become of the people you used to know at school. In particular you remember:
Toni, who used to smoke in the bike sheds in the lunch hour.
Leslie, who used to pull the girls' hair.
Dani, who always chewed gum.

You wonder how they've changed and what they're doing now.

TONI
You are a successful doctor.

You're very curious about what has become of the people you used to know at school. In particular you remember:
Gerry, who always used to have new clothes.
Leslie, who used to pull the girls' hair.
Dani, who always chewed gum.

You wonder how they've changed and what they're doing now.

LESLIE
You are a successful company manager.

You're very curious about what has become of the people you used to know at school. In particular you remember:
Dani, who always chewed gum.
Gerry, who always used to have new clothes.
Terry, who never used to share sweets.

You wonder how they've changed and what they're doing now.

DANI
You are a successful dentist.

You're very curious about what has become of the people you used to know at school. In particular you remember:
Gerry, who always had new clothes.
Terry, who never used to share sweets.
Sam, who used to have a fantastic 10-speed bike.

You wonder how they've changed and what they're doing now.

24 SCHOOL REUNION (Role cards)

GERRY
You are a successful fashion model.

You're very curious about what has become of the people you used to know at school. In particular you remember:
Terry, who never used to share sweets,
Sam, who used to have a fantastic 10-speed bike.
Phil, who used to throw paper darts at the teacher.

You wonder how they've changed and what they're doing now.

TERRY
You are a successful politician.

You're very curious about what has become of the people you used to know at school. In particular you remember:
Alex, who used to be the teacher's pet.
Toni, who used to smoke in the bike sheds in the lunch hour.
Leslie, who used to pull the girls' hair.

You wonder how they've changed and what they're doing now.

SAM
You are a taxi driver.

You're very curious about what has become of the people you used to know at school. In particular you remember:
Dani, who always chewed gum.
Gerry, who always had new clothes.
Phil, who used to throw paper darts at the teacher.

You wonder how they've changed and what they're doing now.

PHIL
You are a soldier.

You're very curious about what has become of the people you used to know at school. In particular you remember:
Terry, who never used to share sweets.
Gerry, who always had new clothes.
Sam, who used to have a fantastic 10-speed bike.

You wonder how they've changed and what they're doing now.

24 SCHOOL REUNION (Role cards)

CHRIS
You are an undertaker.

You're very curious about what has become of the people you used to know at school. In particular you remember:
Phil, who used to throw paper darts at the teacher.
Sam, who had a fantastic 10-speed bike.
Terry, who never shared sweets.

You wonder how they've changed and what they're doing now.

JAN
You are a train driver.

You're very curious about what has become of the people you used to know at school. In particular you remember:
Toni, who used to smoke in the bike sheds in the lunch hour.
Alex, who used to be the teacher's pet.
Chris, who used to play practical jokes.

You wonder how they've changed and what they're doing now.

ROBBIE
You are a vicar.

You're very curious about what has become of the people you used to know at school. In particular you remember:
Toni, who used to smoke in the bike sheds in the lunch hour.
Jan, who always used to be late for everything.
Chris, who used to play practical jokes.

You wonder how they've changed and what they're doing now.

PAUL
You are a dustman.

You're very curious about what has become of the people you used to know at school. In particular you remember:
Chris, who used to play practical jokes.
Jan, who used to be late for everything.
Robbie, who used to be the naughtiest in the class – always getting detentions.

You wonder how they've changed and what they're doing now.

24 SCHOOL REUNION (Role cards)

PIP
You are a teacher.

You're very curious about what has become of the people you used to know at school. In particular you remember:
Paul, who always used to come top in class.
Robbie, who was the naughtiest in the class.
Jan, who always used to be late for everything.

You wonder how they've changed and what they're doing now.

JO
You are a successful TV interviewer with your own chat show.

You're very curious about what has become of the people you used to know at school. In particular you remember:
Pip, who never did any homework.
Paul, who always used to be top of the class.
Robbie, who was the naughtiest in the class.

You wonder how they've changed and what they're doing now.

SIMON/E
You are a secret agent.

You're very curious about what has become of the people you used to know at school. In particular you remember:
Jo, who was always chatting in class.
Pip, who never did any homework.
Paul, who always used to come top.

You wonder how they've changed and what they're doing now.

GLEN/DA
You are a jumbo jet pilot.

You're very curious about what has become of the people you used to know at school. In particular you remember:
Simon/e, who used to tell tales.
Jo, who was very talkative and used to chat in lessons.
Pip, who never did any homework.

You wonder how they've changed and what they're doing now.

24 SCHOOL REUNION (Questionnaire)

Work together to discuss the people you met at the school reunion and to fill in as much of the questionnaire as you can.

ALEX used to ....and now..

TONI used to ....and now..

LESLIE used to ....and now..

DANI used to ....and now..

GERRY used to ....and now..

TERRY never used to ....and now..

SAM used to..and now..

PHIL used to ....and now..

CHRIS used to ....and now..

JAN used to ....and now..

ROBBIE used to...and now..

PAUL used to ....and now..

PIP never used to ....and now..

JO used to...and now..

SIMON/E used to ....and now..

GLEN/DA used to ....and now..

25 LIFEMAP (Board)

Start

Decision 1 — Your parents want you to go to university and study law. Do you go or not? (YES / NO)

Decision 2 — You're looking for a job. They're hard to find. You see an ad for a waiter/waitress. Do you apply? (YES / NO)

Decision 3 — You're unemployed and in debt. A rich uncle offers you flying lessons. You don't like heights. Do you accept? (YES / NO)

Decision 4 — You get a job stacking shelves in a supermarket. One day a customer comes in. He says he's a modernist sculptor and likes your arrangement of soup cans. He recognises your talent and offers you a place at art school. Do you go? (YES / NO)

Decision 4 — You are about to take your pilot's licence. Someone offers you a job at NASA. Do you take it? (YES / NO)

Decision 4 — You hand in your notice. The chief cook invites you to open a casino with him. Do you accept? (YES / NO)

Decision 3 — You get the job. You're bored but you need the money. Do you leave? (YES / NO)

Decision 4 — A customer hears you singing and offers you a job in a nightclub. Do you take it? (YES / NO)

- Ask for card 1
- Ask for card 2
- Ask for card 3
- Ask for card 4
- Ask for card 5
- Ask for card 6
- Ask for card 7
- Ask for card 8
- Ask for card 9
- Ask for card 16

25 LIFEMAP (Board)

LIFEMAP

Ask for card 10

Decision 4 — YES / NO
You become a lawyer. A colleague shows you how to make money by fiddling your expenses. Do you do it?

Ask for card 11

Decision 4 — YES / NO
You get a part as an extra in a film. Then you meet someone, fall in love and want to get married, but they object to your acting career. Do you give it up?

Ask for card 12

Decision 3 — YES / NO
You're a qualified lawyer. You are looking for a job when you meet a 'talent spotter' who is stunned by your good looks and asks you to audition for a film. Do you go?

Decision 2 — LEAVE / STAY
You hate it! Do you leave or stick it out?

Ask for card 13

Decision 4 — YES / NO
You're a police trainee. You don't like it and you're poor. You meet a suspicious-looking character who says he'll give you a lot of money if you help him. Do you agree?

Decision 3 — YES / NO
You're unemployed. It's hard to get a job. You see an ad for the police. Do you apply?

Ask for card 14

Decision 4 — YES / NO
You fall in love with a one-eyed trapeze artist who wants you to join the circus. Do you get married?

Ask for card 15

25 LIFEMAP (Career cards)

1 You became a popstar.

2 You became head waiter.

3 You became a millionaire.

4 You became a tramp.

5 You became an astronaut.

6 You failed your flying exam and became a baggage handler.

7 You became an artist.

8 You became a chief shelf stacker.

9 You became a very successful politician.

10 You got arrested on suspected fraud charges.

11 You became a film star and won four Oscars.

12 You found an office job with a good pension.

13 You became a spy.

14 You became a police officer.

15 You became an acrobat and worked in a circus.

16 You became a bank clerk.

26 HOUSEPARTIES

Ethel (Grandma)
You usually spend Christmas with your son Jim and his wife Edna or your daughter Jean and her husband Pete, but this Christmas you've been thinking you'd like something different. You're fed up with cold damp English Christmases and would really like to go somewhere sunny. You haven't mentioned your idea to anyone yet, and you don't want to offend anyone.... Try talking to your husband George to begin with.

George (Grandpa)
You usually spend Christmas with your son Jim and his wife Edna or your daughter Jean and her husband Pete, but this Christmas you've been thinking you'd like something different. You're fed up with cold damp English Christmases and would really like to go somewhere sunny. You haven't mentioned your idea to anyone yet, and you don't want to offend anyone.... Try talking to your wife Ethel to begin with.

Jean (Mum)
You usually have a big Christmas at home with your kids, Sue, Rob and Paul, your parents George and Ethel and sometimes your brother Jim and his wife Edna. This year you feel you'd like a quiet Christmas at home with your husband Pete and one or two of the young people, maybe, if they want to come (but they're all at university now and might have other ideas – you'd hate them to come out of duty). The difficult thing will be to suggest this tactfully to your parents and brother. Find out how your husband feels first.

Pete (Dad)
Christmas is not your favourite time of year – all that fuss and bother when what you really want to do is to relax at home. You usually have the whole works – a big do with all your wife's family, but this year you'd like a quiet Christmas at home, a couple of the kids around, but not the whole clan!

26 HOUSEPARTIES

Rob
You're very much in love with your girlfriend Sally, and would like to spend Christmas with her – wherever she wants is fine by you!

Sally
You'd like to spend Christmas with your boyfriend Rob – anywhere as long as you're together! You'd be quite happy to go back to his folks, you think his Mum's sweet and his Dad is quite a nice old guy.

Paul
Home is the only place for Christmas!

Sue
You usually have a big family Christmas – grandparents, uncles, aunts, cousins – the lot, but this year you'd like to go skiing with your boyfriend Mick. How are you going to tell your Mum tactfully?

26 HOUSEPARTIES

Edna
You usually have a big Christmas with your parents-in-law, Ethel and George, and your husband's sister Jean and her husband Pete, but this year you'd like to go to Wales with your friends Doris and Ken. You'll have to tell the rest of the family tactfully though – your daughter Avril and her husband Nick, and all your in-laws. Start with your husband Jim.

Jim
You usually have a big Christmas with your parents, Ethel and George, and your sister Jean and her husband Pete, but this year you'd like to do something quieter, perhaps with friends. You'll have to tell the rest of the family tactfully though – your daughter Avril and her husband Nick, and your parents and sister. Start by talking things over with your wife Edna.

Nick
You and your wife Avril got married this year, and you'd like Christmas in your new house. The house is really too small to have people to stay but you'd like open house on Christmas Day – anyone's welcome, the more the merrier.

Avril
You and your husband Nick got married this year and you're really looking forward to your first Christmas in your new house. The trouble is, you usually have a big family Christmas at your parents or your Aunty Jean's house with your grandparents, cousins – the lot. This year you'd really like your own Christmas for a change. There are a lot of foreign students at the college where you teach and some of them might be feeling lonely and left out at Christmas – you'd like to open your house to them. But you need to talk things over with your husband, and then tell your parents tactfully.

26 HOUSEPARTIES

Mick
You'd like to go skiing at Christmas with your girlfriend Sue – but where? It would be fun if a whole group of you could go together.

Sam
Try to get a ski party organised for Christmas with some friends from university. Some French friends have a chalet in the Alps which they would rent to you cheaply. It would take up to eight people.

Tom
A colleague at the office has suggested lending you his villa in Tenerife for the Christmas holidays. You're very excited about the idea, but don't know what your wife Maisie will think. The villa's quite big and you fancy going with some friends – perhaps your old friends George and Ethel would like to go. Try asking your wife first. . .

Maisie
You're fed up with cold damp Christmases and all the extra housework Christmas seems to involve. . . You'd like a Christmas with friends – perhaps your old friends George and Ethel if they'd agree, but you wish it could be somewhere warm!

26 HOUSEPARTIES

Noboru/Masako
You're a Japanese student and this is your first Christmas in England. You might get together with some other foreign students, but you'd really like to know how an English family celebrates Christmas.

Abdul/Sayyida
You're an Omani student and this is your first Christmas in England. You might get together with some other foreign students, but you'd really like to know how an English family celebrates Christmas.

Wai not
You're a Thai student and this is your first Christmas in England. You might get together with some other foreign students, but you'd really like to know how an English family celebrates Christmas.

Sol/Sarah
You're a Namibian student and this is your first Christmas in England. You might get together with some other foreign students, but you'd really like to know how an English family celebrates Christmas.

26 HOUSEPARTIES

Claudio/Claudia
You're an Italian student and this is your first Christmas in England. You might get together with some other foreign students, but you'd really like to know how an English family celebrates Christmas.

Mehmet/Nilgun
You're a Turkish student and this is your first Christmas in England. You might get together with some other foreign students, but you'd really like to know how an English family celebrates Christmas.

Panos/Panayota
You're a Greek student and this is your first Christmas in England. You might get together with some other foreign students, but you'd really like to know how an English family celebrates Christmas.

Jesus-María/María-Jesus
You're a Brazilian student and this is your first Christmas in England. You might get together with some other foreign students, but you'd really like to know how an English family celebrates Christmas.

26 HOUSEPARTIES

Simon/Sandra
You're a university student and would like to go skiing this Christmas. You'd like to join a group of other students if possible.

John/Jane
You're a university student and would like to go skiing this Christmas. You'd like to join a group of other students if possible.

Tim/Tricia
You're a university student and would like to go skiing this Christmas. You'd like to join a group of other students if possible.

Phil/Pauline
You're a university student and would like to go skiing this Christmas. You'd like to join a group of other students if possible.

27 WHEN DID YOU LAST SEE YOUR FATHER?

last week	two years ago	15 years ago	20 years ago
yesterday	the day before yesterday	two days ago	last month
last year	two weeks ago	last summer	two hours ago
10 minutes ago	half an hour ago	last weekend	three days ago
on Sunday morning	this morning	yesterday evening	an hour ago

27 WHEN DID YOU LAST SEE YOUR FATHER?

five years ago	two months ago	10 years ago	last Wednesday

28 THE QUEUE

You were the first person in the queue. You talked about the weather with the person behind you.

You talked about the weather with the person in front of you. The person behind you let you share their umbrella.

You shared your umbrella with the person in front of you. The person behind you caught a train at 6.30 to get in the queue early.

You were very tired as you caught the train at 6.30 to be in the queue early. The person in front of you shared an umbrella with someone else in the queue. The person behind you bought and ate an ice-cream.

You ate an ice-cream while you were waiting. The person in front of you caught a train to be in the queue early. The person behind you had a dog.

You had your dog with you. The person in front of you ate an ice-cream. The person behind you had a lot of shopping bags.

You had a lot of shopping bags with you. The person in front of you had a dog. The person behind you listened to their walkman the whole time.

You listened to music on your walkman while you waited. The person in front of you had a lot of heavy shopping. The person behind you asked you to save their place while they made a telephone call.

You had to make a telephone call and asked people to save your place. The person in front of you listened to a walkman while they were waiting. The person behind you bought a can of coke.

You bought a can of coke to drink while you were waiting. The person in front of you asked you to save their place while they made a telephone call. The person behind you smoked a whole packet of cigarettes.

28 THE QUEUE

You smoked 20 cigarettes while you were waiting. The person in front of you drank a can of coke. The people behind you had an argument.

You quarrelled with your friend in the queue. The person in front of you smoked a lot of cigarettes. The person behind you bought twelve tickets.

You quarrelled with your friend in the queue. The person in front of you smoked a lot of cigarettes. The person behind you bought twelve tickets.

You bought twelve tickets for a school trip. The people in front of you had an argument. The people behind you drank coffee from a thermos.

You and your friend bought a thermos of coffee to drink while you were waiting. The person in front of you bought twelve tickets for the show. The person behind you read a newspaper.

You and your friend bought a thermos of coffee to drink while you were waiting. The person in front of you bought twelve tickets for the show. The person behind you read a newspaper.

You read a newspaper while you waited. The people in front of you drank coffee from a thermos. The person behind you dropped a shopping bag and broke some eggs.

You dropped your shopping bag and broke all the eggs. The person in front of you read a newspaper. The person behind you helped you pick the shopping up.

The person in front of you dropped their shopping bag and the vegetables went all over the pavement. You helped to pick them up. The people behind you sang songs.

The person in front of you helped pick up vegetables from a shopping bag that broke. You and your friend sang songs to stop yourselves getting bored. The person behind you had a heavy suitcase.

28 THE QUEUE

The person in front of you helped pick up vegetables from a shopping bag that broke. You and your friend sang songs to stop yourselves getting bored. The person behind you had a heavy suitcase.

You had just come from the airport and had a very heavy suitcase. The people in front of you got on your nerves: they sang songs all the time. The person behind you wrote postcards.

You wrote postcards to pass the time. The person in front of you had a very heavy suitcase. The person behind you played the guitar.

You played the guitar to pass the time while you waited. The person in front of you wrote several postcards. The people behind you offered everyone a sweet.

You and your friend had a bag of sweets and offered them round. The person in front of you played the guitar. The person behind you ate a hamburger.

You and your friend had a bag of sweets and offered them round. The person in front of you played the guitar. The person behind you ate a hamburger.

You were hungry so you bought a hamburger and ate it standing in the queue. The people in front of you offered everyone some sweets. The person behind you was very impatient and kept looking at their watch.

You had a train to catch and kept looking at your watch. The queue moved very slowly. The person in front of you ate a hamburger. The person behind you whistled an annoying tune.

You whistled to yourself while you waited. The person in front of you was very impatient and kept looking at their watch. The person behind you tried to discuss politics with you.

You tried to discuss politics with the person in front of you, with no success. You were the last person in the queue and when you got to the box office, the tickets were sold out.

29 DETECTIVE WORK (Cards)

At 7 o'clock she went to her sister's house for half an hour.	A friend came to call at 7.45.
By the time her friend knocked on the door she had already started to cook supper.	Her friend stayed to eat supper.
Her friend left shortly after 9 p.m.	She had just said goodbye to her friend when the phone rang.
She had just finished speaking to Uncle Bill on the phone when there was a knock on the door.	Her neighbour wanted to borrow some sugar.
She invited her neighbour in and they chatted until about ten.	She had just said goodbye to her neighbour when the phone rang again. It was her friend, who had forgotten her handbag.

29 DETECTIVE WORK (Cards/Introduction Sheet)

She had just put the phone down when her husband, her son and friend came in.

They had all been to see a film.

After they had had coffee and talked about the film, they all went to bed.

A murder was committed last night. An old lady was found dead in her living room. She had been hit on the head with a frying pan, and jewellery worth £10,000 had been taken from the house. The murder occurred between 7 and 10.30 p.m. One of the principle suspects is Annie Hudson, the district nurse, who has a key to the old lady's house, and who lives ten minutes' walk away.
The cards contain details of Annie's movements that evening. Read them together, and try to work out if she could have committed the murder or not.
Since the cards have been shuffled, the events will be in a muddled order.
Turn up one card at a time from the pile, and talk about *what* happened and *when* it happened: what happened before it, what happened after it.

A murder was committed last night. An old lady was found dead in her living room. She had been hit on the head with a frying pan, and jewellery worth £10,000 had been taken from the house. The murder occurred between 7 and 10.30 p.m. One of the principle suspects is Annie Hudson, the district nurse, who has a key to the old lady's house, and who lives ten minutes' walk away.
The cards contain details of Annie's movements that evening. Read them together, and try to work out if she could have committed the murder or not.
Since the cards have been shuffled, the events will be in a muddled order.
Turn up one card at a time from the pile, and talk about *what* happened and *when* it happened: what happened before it, what happened after it.

A murder was committed last night. An old lady was found dead in her living room. She had been hit on the head with a frying pan, and jewellery worth £10,000 had been taken from the house. The murder occurred between 7 and 10.30 p.m. One of the principle suspects is Annie Hudson, the district nurse, who has a key to the old lady's house, and who lives ten minutes' walk away.
The cards contain details of Annie's movements that evening. Read them together, and try to work out if she could have committed the murder or not.
Since the cards have been shuffled, the events will be in a muddled order.
Turn up one card at a time from the pile, and talk about *what* happened and *when* it happened: what happened before it, what happened after it.

30 SUGGESTIVE SHAPES

31 TACT (Neighbour cards)

Neighbour A
You're fed up with your neighbour's behaviour.
You wish they'd:
>turn their TV down
>keep their dogs out of your back garden
>stop parking in front of your gate

You also wish they'd stop complaining about you: you don't see why *you* should do anything to change *your* lifestyle.

Neighbour B
You're fed up with your neighbour's behaviour.
You wish they'd:
>prevent their teenagers from having late night parties
>chop down the big tree in their garden
>pick their baby up when it cries instead of letting him scream

You also wish they'd stop complaining about you: you don't see why *you* should do anything to change *your* lifestyle.

Go-between
You have to carry messages from one person to the other. Your object is to get them to reach an agreement, but you must report exactly what they said to each other.

31 TACT (Husband and wife cards)

Husband
You wish your wife would:
- stop complaining
- have dinner ready every evening when you come home
- stop quarrelling with your mother

But you don't see why *you* should change anything about *your* lifestyle.

Wife
You wish your husband would:
- help in the house occasionally
- look after the children sometimes
- talk to you in the evenings instead of slumping in front of the telly

But you don't see why *you* should change anything about *your* lifestyle.

Go-between
You have to carry messages from one person to the other. Your object is to get them to reach an agreement, but you must report exactly what they said to each other.

31 TACT (Country cards)

Paranoia
Your neighbouring country Neurotica is causing a lot of problems:
- they are illegally occupying part of your territory on the eastern border
- they are destroying large areas of rain forest, which is causing flooding and damage to land in your country
- their high taxes on food imports are crippling your economy

You don't want to start a war: you'd prefer to solve these problems through negotiation. At the same time, you don't want to give way on any issues.

Neurotica
Your neighbouring country Paranoia is causing a lot of problems:
- they are illegally occupying part of your territory on the western border
- they have built a nuclear power plant near the border
- they have a ban on car imports (your main industry)

You don't want to start a war: you'd prefer to solve these problems through negotiation. At the same time, you don't want to give way on any issues.

Go-between
You have to carry messages from one country to the other. Your object is to get them to reach an agreement, but you must report exactly what they said to each other.

32 YUPPIES

33 ARCHAEOLOGISTS

pre-modern era, c. 1980: child's toy? 	pre-modern era, c. 1970: hair ornament? 	pre-modern era, c. 1950: child's toy? 
early modern era, c. 3000: brooch? 	pre-modern era, c. 2000: religious object? 	early modern era, c. 3000: woman's purse? 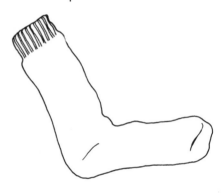
pre-modern era, c. 2200: cooking implement? 	pre-modern era, c. 2100: household decoration? 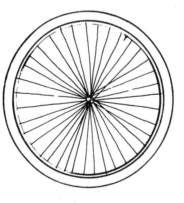	pre-modern era, c. 1960: writing implement? 
pre-modern era, c. 2000: decorative object? 	early modern era, c. 3500: musical instrument? 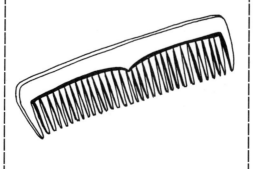	early modern era, c. 2300: item of jewellery? 

34 CRYSTAL BALLS (Hunter cards/Crystal ball)

You want some good news about your love life.

You want some good news about money matters.

You want some good news about your future family (you want lots of children).

You want some exciting news about travel.

You want an interesting career.

You want to be famous.

You want good news about your health.

You are a specialist in **love**. Predict a good / interesting love life for everyone you meet. Be inventive! If they ask you about other things, say that the ball is cloudy and you can't see.

34 CRYSTAL BALLS (Crystal balls)

You are a specialist in **money matters**. Predict a good financial future for everyone you meet. Be inventive! If they ask you about other things, say that the ball is cloudy and you can't see.

You are a specialist in **family life**. Predict a happy family life and large numbers of children for everyone you meet. Be inventive! If they ask you about other things, say that the ball is cloudy and you can't see.

34 CRYSTAL BALLS (Crystal balls)

You are a specialist in **travel.** Predict interesting travel experiences for everyone you meet. Be inventive! If they ask you about other things, say that the ball is cloudy and you can't see.

You are a **career** specialist. Predict an interesting/successful career for everyone you meet. Be inventive! If they ask you about other things, say that the ball is cloudy and you can't see.

34 CRYSTAL BALLS (Crystal balls)

You are a specialist in **fame**. Predict success and fame for everyone you meet. Be inventive! If they ask you about other things, say that the ball is cloudy and you can't see.

You are a specialist in **health**. Predict a healthy life and vigorous old age for everyone you meet. Be inventive! If they ask you about other things, say that the ball is cloudy and you can't see.

35 CHRISTMAS SWAPPING

This Christmas you were given three pairs of hiking socks and a flower arranging book. What a waste! You *hate* hiking and *loathe* flower arranging. What you really like is ballet and pottering about in the house doing a spot of DIY. You're not an outdoor type at all.

Your hobby is flower arranging – and your passion is hiking in the mountains – you go off every holiday and most weekends if you can. But what did you get for Christmas? Two tickets for the ballet and a book on DIY! You really dislike ballet and DIY is your pet hate! Someone should send Father Christmas for re-training!

This Christmas you got a classical music cassette – dreary stuff, Borg, Buck, Buch or something. You can't stand classical music and never listen to it. What you like is jazz. The other present you got was equally dreary – a boring book – some modern novel. Reading never was your strong point – can't seem to find time for it anyway these days. If people can't think what to send, why don't they send something to eat – that always goes down well!

This Christmas you got a jazz cassette and a box of chocolates. Very nice too, except you like classical music, and you're trying to slim! What you really wanted for Christmas was books.

35 CHRISTMAS SWAPPING

This Christmas you got a tennis racquet and two tickets to the opera. What's wrong with Santa these days? Wrong sport for a start. You play golf, not tennis, and you've always hated opera – pop music is what you like.

This Christmas you got a pop record and a set of golf balls. Santa must have got the wrong file out when he was making that decision! You like opera, not pop, and tennis is your sport, not golf!

This Christmas, Santa awarded you a set of saucepans and an apron! What a mistake! You're not a feminist, but you don't really see why *women* always get the boring saucepans and household stuff. What you'd like is something frilly, glamorous and totally frivolous. Saucepans you can buy for yourself!

This Christmas you got not one, but *two* sets of frilly French underwear! What a waste! How can people spend their money on something so frivolous? You've just moved into a new house and money is really tight. What you need is something practical for the house. Knickers to underwear!

35 CHRISTMAS SWAPPING

This Christmas Santa sent you a set of gardening tools and a book on houseplant care. Santa needs his head examined! You *hate* gardening – it's just like outdoor housework to you. And every houseplant you've ever been given has died a very nasty death. In fact you're not interested in plants or the outdoor life, or anything remotely green. What you like is games – board games, card games – you name it!

This Christmas, for some unknown reason, a misguided Father Christmas brought you a chess book and computer bridge. You've never played either game in your life and you don't intend to start now! In fact you don't like being indoors at all – what you love is gardening and plants.

This Christmas Santa gave you a bottle of Chanel No. 5 perfume. Very nice, and probably very expensive, but the problem is you don't *like* Chanel No.5. You like Dior. The other present you got was an English-Turkish dictionary. Very strange, you thought, until you realised that you'd told everyone where you were going for your holiday. They thought you'd said Turkey – but actually you'd said *Torquay*.

This Christmas Santa gave you a bottle of Dior perfume. Very nice too – but what a waste. Your perfume is Chanel No.5. You never wear any other. And you also got a guide to Torquay. This mystified you until you realised that people had misunderstood where you're going on holiday. You're going to *Turkey*.

35 CHRISTMAS SWAPPING

In your Christmas stocking was a cook book and a gift pack of Indian spices. Maybe Santa's dropping a hint, but it won't work. You hate cooking. And your pet hate is Indian food. In fact you don't like any indoor hobbies at all. Your hobby is watersports.

You really can't understand it. For Christmas you got a snorkel and a wetsuit. You can't swim. In fact you're aquaphobic. You don't like sports at all. Your favourite hobby is cooking. You've just started a course in Indian cookery.

For Christmas you received a print of an Impressionist painting, and a book on astronomy. Well, it was nearly right. You like art, and you're fascinated by the stars. The only problem is that the Impressionists are your pet hate – you prefer abstract painting, and it's *astrology*, not astronomy, you're interested in!

For Christmas, you received a book on astrology and a Mondrian print. Well, it was nearly right. You like art and you're fascinated by the stars. The only problem is that you hate abstract painting, and it's *astronomy*, not astrology that you're interested in!

35 CHRISTMAS SWAPPING

This Christmas you had a really original present. Socks and handkerchiefs! Boring! You *were* hoping for some videos – you've just bought a video machine.

This Christmas you got two videos as presents. You don't even have a television! What a waste of time! You wish people would give *useful* presents – clothes for example.

This Christmas you got a guitar complete with 'Teach Yourself' manual. Did no one tell Santa you were tone-deaf? You're not in the slightest interested in music. Your hobby is genealogy.

What you really hoped for this Christmas was a guitar. You want to start guitar lessons at the local college this January. The problem is, you can't afford a guitar. So what did you get?....... A book called *Trace Your Own Family History*.

36 HEADS, BODIES AND LEGS

36 HEADS, BODIES AND LEGS

36 HEADS, BODIES AND LEGS

37 THE ADVERB GAME

passionately	violently	secretly	slowly
loudly	happily	softly	angrily
sadly	noisily	anxiously	uncomfortably
strictly	gently	regretfully	timidly
boldly	tenderly	tearfully	politely
rudely	quickly	nervously	disapprovingly

38 BOILED EGGS

1 How do you like your eggs boiled?
Arrange yourselves in a line:

runny ------------------------------ hard

2 How big are your feet?
Arrange yourselves in a line:

big ------------------------------ small

3 What is your favourite time of day?
Arrange yourselves in a line:

early morning ------------------ late night

4 How many hours of TV do you watch a day?
Arrange yourselves in a line:

none ------------------------------ 24

39 MARRIED LIFE (Cards)

39 MARRIED LIFE (Diaries)

Monday 27 January

8·00 drive kids to school

11·00 dentist

1·00 lunch with Susie and Jeff

4·00 parents' meeting at school

7·00 guitar class

Monday 27 January

8·00 drive kids to school

11·00 dentist

1·00 lunch with Susie and Jeff

4·00 parents' meeting at school

7·00 guitar class

Monday 27 January

10·00 meeting

1·00 lunch with Jo

4·00 parents' meeting

8·00 Art class

10·30 pick Mum up from station

Monday 27 January

10·00 meeting

1·00 lunch with Jo

4·00 parents' meeting

8·00 Art class

10·30 pick Mum up from station

39 MARRIED LIFE (Board)

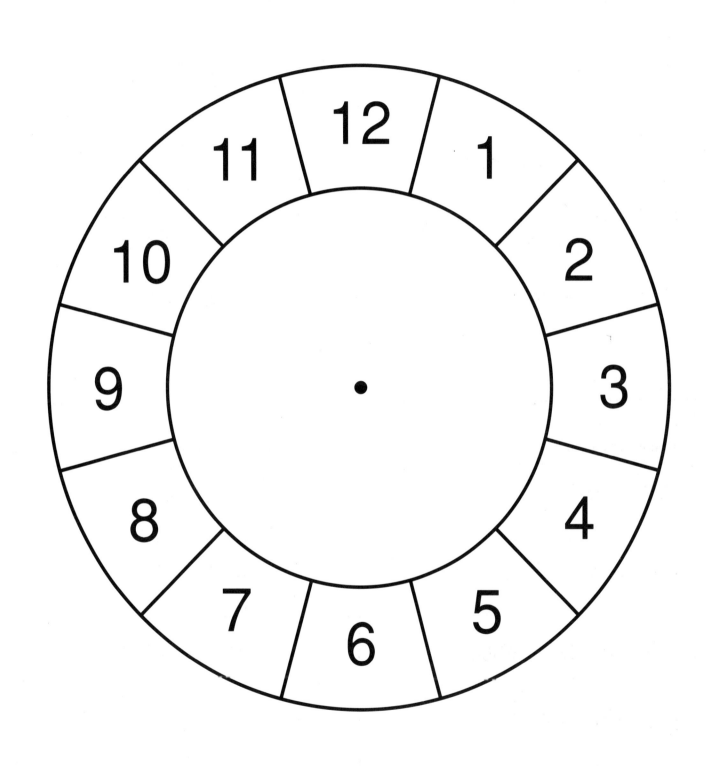

40 THE LAST GAME

Find someone you would like to thank for:

wearing colourful clothes

making you laugh

being even later for class than you were

having a name you could pronounce

telling you something interesting about their country

having a nice smile

being cheerful on a Monday morning

telling you the answers you didn't know

telling jokes

lending you things you'd forgotten

being enthusiastic

always speaking English to you

enjoying life

being helpful

being friendly

Find someone you would like to thank for:

wearing colourful clothes

making you laugh

being even later for class than you were

having a name you could pronounce

telling you something interesting about their country

having a nice smile

being cheerful on a Monday morning

telling you the answers you didn't know

telling jokes

lending you things you'd forgotten

being enthusiastic

always speaking English to you

enjoying life

being helpful

being friendly

RULES SHEETS (4, 9, 12^A, 12^B)

4 Relatively speaking
Rules
1. Play this game in groups of three or four.
2. Place the picture cards face down in a pile in the middle of the table.
3. Player 1: take the top card from the pile. Look at it, but don't show it to the others!
4. Player 1 gives a definition of the place, person or machine on his/her card. For example, for a picture of a hospital, *This is a place where you go when you're sick.* Or, if you want to make it more difficult for the others to guess, you can say, *This is a place where nice people bring you tea in bed.*
5. The other players must try to guess the name of the place, person or machine.
6. The first player to guess correctly can keep the card.
7. If no one can guess, player 1 can keep the card.
8. Then it is the next player's turn.
9. The player with most cards at the end is the winner.

9 Sci-fi dominoes/Fairytale dominoes
Rules
1. Play this game in groups of three or four.
2. Deal out the cards equally to each player.
3. Look at your cards. These represent the events in a science fiction story/fairytale.
4. Player 1: choose any card and lay it down on the table. This is the first event in the story. Tell the others what happened.
5. Player 2: choose a card and lay it down next to the first one, and tell the others what happened next.
6. The aim of the game is to build up a story together.

12 Good news, bad news (A)
Rules
1. Play this game in groups of three or four.
2. Deal out the cards equally to each player.
3. Some cards are labelled 'GN' (good news) and some are labelled 'BN' (bad news).
4. Player 1: choose a good news card. Put it down on the table saying *The good news is ...* and describing what happened, for example *The good news is, I asked my girlfriend to marry me.*
5. The other players must look for a bad news card that follows this and put it on the table saying, *The bad news is ...*, for example, *The bad news is, she refused.*
6. The player who finds the right 'bad news' can collect both cards and keep them on the table.
7. At the end, the player with most cards on the table is the winner.

12 Good news, bad news (B)
Rules
1. Play this game in groups of three or four.
2. One player is the quizmaster and keeps the sheet of pictures without showing it to the others.
3. The quizmaster looks at the first picture and describes what happened, beginning, *The good news is....*, for example, *The good news is, I asked my girlfriend to marry me.*
4. The other players must guess what the 'bad news' is, for example, *The bad news is, I asked the wrong girl/The bad news is, she didn't listen/The bad news is, she refused.*
5. If a player guesses correctly, the quizmaster gives them a point.
6. The player with the most points at the end of the game is the winner.

RULES SHEETS (14, 18ᴀ, 18ᴮ, 23)

14 Future snap
Rules
1. Play this game in groups of three or four.
2. Shuffle the cards and deal them out equally to all players.
3. Player 1: choose the first half of a sentence, read it out to the others and put it on the table.
4. The other players must try to find a good second half for the sentence. The complete sentence must make sense and it must be grammatically correct. If you disagree, call your teacher!
5. The first player to find a suitable second half-sentence can collect the two half sentences and keep them as a 'trick'.
6. The player with most 'tricks' at the end is the winner.

18 Yuck! (A)
Rules
1. Play this game in pairs.
2. Student A has a sheet of pictures. Do not show them to student B.
3. Student B has the same pictures, cut up.
4. Student A must describe the pictures in order to student B.
   Do not say the names of the pictures. Say *It makes me...*, for example, *It makes me hot*, *It makes me feel sad*.
5. Student B must arrange the pictures in the same order. You can ask questions, for example, *Does it make you wet? Does it make you look nice?*

18 Yuck! (B)
Rules
1. Play this game in groups of three or four.
2. Place the pictures face down in a pile in the middle. Do not look at them.
3. Player 1: take the first picture from the pile and look at it. Do not show it to the others.
4. Say something about the picture, beginning, *It makes me...*, for example, *It makes me cold and wet* or *It makes me feel uncomfortable*.
5. The other players must try to guess what the picture is. They may ask questions, for example, *Does it make you sad?* or *Does it make you look nice?*
6. The player who guesses correctly can keep the card and take the next picture from the pile.
7. The player with most cards at the end is the winner.

23 Guess what I've been doing!
Rules
1. Play this game in groups of three or four.
2. Put the pictures face down in the middle of the table.
3. Player 1: take the top picture but don't show it to the others! Imagine you are the person in the picture. Describe your **appearance** to the others, but do **not** say what you have been doing. (For example, you can say *I'm crying,* but not *I've been peeling onions.*)
4. The other players must try to guess what you have been doing, for example, *You've been listening to a sad song*.
5. The player who guesses correctly can keep the picture card, and gets the next turn.
6. At the end, the player with the most cards is the winner.

RULES SHEETS (25, 27)

25 Lifemap
Rules
1. Play this game in groups of three or four.
2. Place your counters on START.
3. First player: throw the dice and move your counter forward. As soon as you come to a DECISION SQUARE you must stop, even if you haven't finished.
4. Read what it says on the DECISION SQUARE and ask the other players for advice (*What shall I do?* or *What do you think I should do?*).
5. They must tell you what they think you should do (*You should..., I think you ought to...*).
6. You must do what the group decides. If you can't agree, call your teacher to vote.
7. When the group has decided what you should do, you must move in the direction you have chosen. If your turn isn't finished, you can finish it, otherwise, wait till the next turn.
8. Then it is the next player's turn.
9. Every time someone comes to a DECISION SQUARE you must stop and ask the rest of the group for advice.
10. When you get to the circle at the end, ask the teacher for the card with that number on, and you will discover what finally happened to you!

27 When did you last see your father?
Rules
1. Play this game in groups of three or four.
2. There are two sets of cards: picture cards and time cards.
3. Deal out the time cards to each player.
4. Put the picture cards face down in the middle of the table.
5. Player 1: take a picture card from the top of the pile and ask the player on your right a question beginning *When did you first...?* or *When did you last....?* For example if you pick up the picture of a TV you can ask *When did you first watch TV?* or *When did you last watch TV?*
6. The player on your right must answer using one of the time cards, for example, *Yesterday evening* or *Fifteen years ago*.
7. The other players must decide if they believe the answer. (The answer doesn't have to be exactly true, just believable. For example, *Yesterday evening* sounds likely, but *Fifteen years ago* doesn't.)
8. If you think the answer sounds convincing, the player may throw away the time card.
9. If you don't believe the player, you can challenge him/her. Then he/she must tell the truth, and keep the time card.
10. Then it is the next player's turn to pick up a picture card.
11. The player who gets rid of all the time cards first is the winner.

RULES SHEETS (30, 32, 33, 37)

30 Suggestive shapes
Rules
1. Play this game in pairs.
2. Student A has a sheet of pictures. Do not show them to student B.
3. Student B has the same pictures, cut up.
4. Student A must describe the pictures in order to student B. (for example, *It could be a hat, It might be a potato*, etc.)
5. Student B must arrange the pictures in the same order.

32 Yuppies
Rules
1. Play this game in groups of three or four.
2. Shuffle the cards and deal them out equally.
3. The first player should choose a card and lay it on the table saying something about it, for example *My car cost £50,000*.
4. The next player should choose a card and lay it down next to the first player's card, making a comparison, for example, *My ring was more expensive than your car*.
5. The third player should put another card down next to the second player's card, making a comparison such as, *My wife is more beautiful than your ring*.
6. The next player should do the same, for example, *My dog has a nicer personality than your wife*.
7. And so on.
8. If a player cannot think of a comparison, the turn passes to the next player.
9. The first player to finish is the winner.
10. *But* you mustn't use any adjectives more than once.
11. *And* nonsense (*My house is more intelligent than your car*) is not permitted.

33 Archaeologists
Rules
1. Play this game in groups of three or four.
2. Place the picture cards face down in a pile in the middle of the group. Do not look at them.
3. You are all archaeologists in the year 5000. The picture cards are objects that you have discovered, but you are not sure what they were used for.
4. First archaeologist: take the first card from the pile, but don't show it to the others.
5. Read the information on the top of the card to the others and then describe the appearance of the object (shape, size, what it's made of). Don't say its name!
6. If any of the other archaeologists think they know what the object was *really* used for, they should tell you.
7. If they guess correctly, give them the card to keep.
8. If they are wrong, you may keep the card.
9. Then it is the next player's turn.
10. The player with most cards at the end is winner.

37 The adverb game
Rules
1. Play this game in groups of three or four.
2. Place the cards face down in a pile in the centre of the group.
3. First player: take the top card but don't show it to the others.
4. Try to help the others to guess the adverb without saying the word. For example if you have 'GENTLY', you can say *You stroke a cat like this* or *You speak to a baby like this*.
5. Then the others must try to guess the word. They can ask a question, for example, *Can you sing like this?* or *Can you walk like this?*
6. The player who guesses correctly can keep the card.
7. Then it is the next player's turn.
8. The player with most cards at the end of the game is the winner.

39 Married life *or* Getting out of doing the washing-up
Rules
1. Play this game in pairs.
2. You will need a board, a set of picture cards, a diary each, two counters and a dice.
3. Put the board on the table between you, and put both your counters at 12 o'clock.
4. Put the picture cards face down in a pile in the middle.
5. Take a diary each. *Don't* show it to the other person.
6. Student A begins. Throw the dice and move your counter round to a different 'time' on the clock, according to the number you have thrown.
7. Take the top card from the pile.
8. Imagine you and your partner are a married couple, who don't like housework, and the picture on the card is something that needs doing in your house. Ask your partner to do it. Say, for example, *Darling, could you do the washing-up, please* or *It's your turn to do the washing-up* or *It's about time you did the washing-up for a change, isn't it?*
9. Student B: look at your diary. If you have an appointment for that time, you can make an excuse. Say *Sorry, but I've got to go to the dentist's* or *I must get ready for my cookery class*. But if you have no appointment for that time, you can either: 1) tell the truth: agree to do the job and take the card or 2) bluff – pretend you've got an appointment: say *Sorry I've got to go to the dentist's* (even if it's not true!).
10. Student A: if student B agrees to do the job, give him/her the card. Then it's student B's turn to throw the dice.
    But if he/she makes an excuse, you must decide if he/she's telling the truth. If you think he/she's telling the truth then say *OK, I'll do it*: you keep the card and it's student B's turn to throw the dice.
    If you think he/she's not telling the truth, challenge him/her. Say *I don't believe you*. If you're right, then student B has to keep the card *and* miss a turn. But if you're wrong then *you* have to keep the card *and* miss a turn!
11. The player with the fewest cards at the end of the game is the winner.

---

39 Married life *or* Getting out of doing the washing-up
Rules
1. Play this game in pairs.
2. You will need a board, a set of picture cards, a diary each, two counters and a dice.
3. Put the board on the table between you, and put both your counters at 12 o'clock.
4. Put the picture cards face down in a pile in the middle.
5. Take a diary each. *Don't* show it to the other person.
6. Student A begins. Throw the dice and move your counter round to a different 'time' on the clock, according to the number you have thrown.
7. Take the top card from the pile.
8. Imagine you and your partner are a married couple, who don't like housework, and the picture on the card is something that needs doing in your house. Ask your partner to do it. Say, for example, *Darling, could you do the washing-up, please* or *It's your turn to do the washing-up* or *It's about time you did the washing-up for a change, isn't it?*
9. Student B: look at your diary. If you have an appointment for that time, you can make an excuse. Say *Sorry, but I've got to go to the dentist's* or *I must get ready for my cookery class*. But if you have no appointment for that time, you can either: 1) tell the truth: agree to do the job and take the card or 2) bluff – pretend you've got an appointment: say *Sorry I've got to go to the dentist's* (even if it's not true!).
10. Student A: if student B agrees to do the job, give him/her the card. Then it's student B's turn to throw the dice.
    But if he/she makes an excuse, you must decide if he/she's telling the truth. If you think he/she's telling the truth then say *OK, I'll do it*: you keep the card and it's student B's turn to throw the dice.
    If you think he/she's not telling the truth, challenge him/her. Say *I don't believe you*. If you're right, then student B has to keep the card *and* miss a turn. But if you're wrong then *you* have to keep the card *and* miss a turn!
11. The player with the fewest cards at the end of the game is the winner.

INDEX

Structural index

Note that the numbers refer to the games.

adjectives
   character 17
   feelings 5, 18
   material 33
   objects 30, 33
   people 36
   places 11
   shape 33, 36
   size 33, 36
   comparison of 32, 38

ago 27

adverbs
   manner 37
   time 14, 27

be 6, 10, 17, 32, 33, 36

be able 19

can
   possibility 37
   requests 39
   ability 19

comparatives 32, 38

conditions
   first 21, 31
   second 16
   third 25

could
   ability 3
   requests 39
   possibility 30

future continuous 14

future perfect 14

have got 2, 10, 11, 33, 36

have to 39
   will/won't have to 19

gerund 2, 40

going to 13, 14, 26

might 30

must 39
   (see also *have to*)

need 11

ought to 15, 25

ought to have 15

passives
   past 20
   present 33

past continuous 8, 9

past perfect 9, 29

past simple 8, 9, 12, 22, 27, 28, 29

present continuous
   for fixed arrangements 14, 26
   for habits 1
   for present situations 24

present perfect 22

present perfect continuous 23

present simple 1, 5, 7, 37

questions
   wh— 1, 5, 6, 7, 8, 10, 22, 24, 25, 27, 34
   yes/no 1, 2, 5, 7, 10, 13, 18, 20, 21,
   22, 23, 28, 30, 34, 36, 37, 38

relative clauses 2, 4, 7
   where 4
   which 2, 4
   who 4
   whose 7
   with end prepositions 2

reported speech 31

shall 25

should 15, 25

should have 15

superlatives 38

time clauses 14

used to 24

verb +—ing 1, 6, 22, 35

verb + object + infinitive 18

was going to 13

will
   prediction 15, 34
   promises 21
   pure future 14
   arrangements 26

will be able to 19

will be —ing 14

will have —ed 14, 34

wish 3

won't have to 19

would like/rather/prefer 5, 6, 11, 26

Lexical index

Note that this index deals with lexical areas, rather than specific items of vocabulary. The numbers refer to the games.

abilities 3, 17
academic subjects 1
appointments 10, 39
bodies 36, 38
career choices 25, 34
childhood 20, 24
clothes 36
crime 22, 29
daily life 5, 15
decisions 25
dentist 10
doctor 10
entertainment 10
everyday activities 8, 12, 13, 14, 16, 23, 27, 28, 29, 37,
fairytale, fantasy 9
family life 7, 20, 21, 31, 34, 38
feelings 18
habits 1, 24, 38
health 34
hobbies and interests 1, 6, 7, 22, 35
holidays 26
household tasks 19, 20, 39
houses 5, 11
international affairs 31
leisure interests 26
lifestyle 5, 11
likes and dislikes 7, 38
love 34, 3
machines 4
money 34, 3
musical instruments 1
neighbours 31
noises 1
objects 30, 33
obligations 19, 39
occupations 4, 24, 25, 34
people
   appearance 36, 38
   personality 3, 17
personal characteristics 3, 17, 40
pets 7
places 4
possessions 3, 32
problems 15
quarrels 31
schooldays 24
science fiction 8, 9
services 10
sports 1, 6, 7, 22, 35
talents 3, 17
thanks 40
tools 2, 4
travel 22, 34
utensils 2